ECONOMIC ISSUES, PROBLEMS AND PERSPECTIVES

AF764419

BUDGETARY AND ECONOMIC OUTLOOKS TO 2023 AND THEIR MACROECONOMIC EFFECTS

ECONOMIC ISSUES, PROBLEMS AND PERSPECTIVES

Additional books in this series can be found on Nova's website under the Series tab.

Additional E-books in this series can be found on Nova's website under the E-book tab.

ECONOMIC ISSUES, PROBLEMS AND PERSPECTIVES

BUDGETARY AND ECONOMIC OUTLOOKS TO 2023 AND THEIR MACROECONOMIC EFFECTS

LIAM KRAUSE
EDITOR

NOVINKA

New York

Copyright © 2013 by Nova Science Publishers, Inc.

All rights reserved. No part of this book may be reproduced, stored in a retrieval system or transmitted in any form or by any means: electronic, electrostatic, magnetic, tape, mechanical photocopying, recording or otherwise without the written permission of the Publisher.

For permission to use material from this book please contact us:
Telephone 631-231-7269; Fax 631-231-8175
Web Site: http://www.novapublishers.com

NOTICE TO THE READER

The Publisher has taken reasonable care in the preparation of this book, but makes no expressed or implied warranty of any kind and assumes no responsibility for any errors or omissions. No liability is assumed for incidental or consequential damages in connection with or arising out of information contained in this book. The Publisher shall not be liable for any special, consequential, or exemplary damages resulting, in whole or in part, from the readers' use of, or reliance upon, this material. Any parts of this book based on government reports are so indicated and copyright is claimed for those parts to the extent applicable to compilations of such works.

Independent verification should be sought for any data, advice or recommendations contained in this book. In addition, no responsibility is assumed by the publisher for any injury and/or damage to persons or property arising from any methods, products, instructions, ideas or otherwise contained in this publication.

This publication is designed to provide accurate and authoritative information with regard to the subject matter covered herein. It is sold with the clear understanding that the Publisher is not engaged in rendering legal or any other professional services. If legal or any other expert assistance is required, the services of a competent person should be sought. FROM A DECLARATION OF PARTICIPANTS JOINTLY ADOPTED BY A COMMITTEE OF THE AMERICAN BAR ASSOCIATION AND A COMMITTEE OF PUBLISHERS.

Additional color graphics may be available in the e-book version of this book.

LIBRARY OF CONGRESS CATALOGING-IN-PUBLICATION DATA

ISBN: 978-1-62618-760-3

Published by Nova Science Publishers, Inc. † New York

CONTENTS

PREFACE

If current laws remain in place, the Congressional Budget Office (CBO) estimates, the federal budget deficit will total $845 billion in fiscal year 2013; this will be the first time since 2008 that the budget shortfall will be less than $1 trillion. At 5.3 percent of gross domestic product (GDP), that deficit will be well below the peak of 10.1 percent in 2009 but still larger than in all by one year between 1947 and 2008. As a result, debt held by the public is estimated to increase to 76 percent of GDP by the end of 2013, the largest ratio since 1950. This book examines the budgetary and economic outlooks to fiscal year 2023 and their macroeconomic effects.

Chapter 1 – Economic growth will remain slow this year, the Congressional Budget Office (CBO) anticipates, as gradual improvement in many of the forces that drive the economy is offset by the effects of budgetary changes that are scheduled to occur under current law. After this year, economic growth will speed up, CBO projects, causing the unemployment rate to decline and inflation and interest rates to eventually rise from their current low levels. Nevertheless, the unemployment rate is expected to remain above 71/2 percent through next year; if that happens, 2014 will be the sixth consecutive year with unemployment exceeding 71/2 percent of the labor force—the longest such period in the past 70 years. If the current laws that govern federal taxes and spending do not change, the budget deficit will shrink this year to $845 billion, or 5.3 percent of gross domestic product (GDP), its smallest size since 2008. In CBO's baseline projections, deficits continue to shrink over the next few years, falling to 2.4 percent of GDP by 2015. Deficits are projected to increase later in the coming decade, however, because of the pressures of an aging population, rising health care costs, an expansion of federal subsidies for health insurance, and growing interest payments on federal debt. As a result, federal debt held by the public is projected to remain historically high relative to the size of the economy for the next decade. By 2023, if current laws remain in place, debt will equal 77 percent of GDP and be on an upward path, CBO projects (see Summary Figure 1). Such high and rising debt would have serious negative consequences: When interest rates rose to more normal levels, federal spending on interest payments would increase substantially. Moreover, because federal borrowing reduces national saving, the capital stock would be smaller and total wages would be lower than they would be if the debt was reduced. In addition, lawmakers would have less flexibility than they might ordinarily to use tax and spending policies to respond to unexpected challenges. Finally, such a large debt would increase the risk of a fiscal crisis, during which investors would lose so much confidence in the government's ability to manage its budget that the government would be unable to borrow at affordable rates.

Chapter 2 - Federal debt held by the public now exceeds 70 percent of the nation's annual output (gross domestic product, or GDP) and stands at a higher percentage than in any year since 1950. Under an assumption whereby current laws generally remain unchanged, federal debt will be 77 percent of GDP in 2023, the Congressional Budget Office (CBO) projects. Such a large amount of federal debt will reduce the nation's output and income below what would occur if the debt was smaller, and it raises the risk of a fiscal crisis (in which the government would lose the ability to borrow money at affordable interest rates). Moreover, the aging of the population and rising health care costs will tend to push debt even higher in the following decades.

In addition, those projections of debt under current law incorporate scheduled changes in policies that will serve to restrain the growth of debt. For example, under current law, some significant tax provisions will expire at the end of this year or in later years, increasing revenues; automatic spending cuts included in the Budget Control Act of 2011 and modified in the American Taxpayer Relief Act of 2012 will go into effect on March 1, 2013; and Medicare's payment rates for physicians' services will fall in Jnuary 2014. If future legislation prevented those changes from taking effect and did not make other policy changes with offsetting budgetary effects, federal debt would be considerably higher than the amount projected under current law.

To aid lawmakers in assessing the macroeconomic effects of possible changes in tax and spending policies, this report describes the effects of three alternative budgetary paths: one with deficits that are greater than those projected under current law and two with deficits that are smaller. Those paths are purely illustrative and do not represent recommendations by CBO.

In evaluating policy changes that would change projected budget deficits, lawmakers would undoubtedly weigh other considerations besides the macroeconomic effects—taking into account, for example, views about the proper size of the federal government and the best allocation of its resources. Lawmakers would also be concerned about the distributional implications of proposed changes—that is, who would bear the burden of any cuts in spending or increases in taxes (or who would benefit from spending increases or tax cuts), and who would gain or lose from changes in economic conditions. Such considerations are outside the scope of this analysis but have been addressed by CBO in other reports.

In: Budgetary and Economic Outlooks to 2023 ... ISBN: 978-1-62618-760-3
Editor: Liam Krause © 2013 Nova Science Publishers, Inc.

Chapter 1

THE BUDGET AND ECONOMIC OUTLOOK: FISCAL YEARS 2013 TO 2023*

Christina Hawley Anthony, Barry Blom, Mark Booth, Charles Whalen, Amber Marcellino, Jessica Banthin and Alexander Arnon

NOTES

Numbers in the text and tables may not add up to totals because of rounding.

Unless otherwise indicated, years referred to in describing the budget outlook are federal fiscal years (which run from October 1 to September 30) and years referred to in describing the economic outlook are calendar years.

Figures 2-1 through 2-5 have white vertical bars that indicate the duration of recessions. (A recession extends from the peak of a business cycle to its trough.)

The economic forecast was completed in mid-January 2013, and the estimates of 2012 values shown in Tables 2-1 through 2-4 and Figures 2-1 through 2-5 and Appendix B are based on information available at that time.

---

* Christina Hawley Anthony, Barry Blom, Mark Booth, Charles Whalen, Amber Marcellino, Jessica Banthin, and Alexander Arnon wrote this report which was released by the Congressional Budget Office.

Supplemental data for this analysis and the historical budget data that are usually included in this report are available on CBO's Web site (www.cbo.gov).

SUMMARY

Economic growth will remain slow this year, the Congressional Budget Office (CBO) anticipates, as gradual improvement in many of the forces that drive the economy is offset by the effects of budgetary changes that are scheduled to occur under current law. After this year, economic growth will speed up, CBO projects, causing the unemployment rate to decline and inflation and interest rates to eventually rise from their current low levels. Nevertheless, the unemployment rate is expected to remain above 71/2 percent through next year; if that happens, 2014 will be the sixth consecutive year with unemployment exceeding 71/2 percent of the labor force—the longest such period in the past 70 years. If the current laws that govern federal taxes and spending do not change, the budget deficit will shrink this year to $845 billion, or 5.3 percent of gross domestic product (GDP), its smallest size since 2008. In CBO's baseline projections, deficits continue to shrink over the next few years, falling to 2.4 percent of GDP by 2015. Deficits are projected to increase later in the coming decade, however, because of the pressures of an aging population, rising health care costs, an expansion of federal subsidies for health insurance, and growing interest payments on federal debt. As a result, federal debt held by the public is projected to remain historically high relative to the size of the economy for the next decade. By 2023, if current laws remain in place, debt will equal 77 percent of GDP and be on an upward path, CBO projects (see Summary Figure 1). Such high and rising debt would have serious negative consequences: When interest rates rose to more normal levels, federal spending on interest payments would increase substantially. Moreover, because federal borrowing reduces national saving, the capital stock would be smaller and total wages would be lower than they would be if the debt was reduced. In addition, lawmakers would have less flexibility than they might ordinarily to use tax and spending policies to respond to unexpected challenges. Finally, such a large debt would increase the risk of a fiscal crisis, during which investors would lose so much confidence in the government's ability to manage its budget that the government would be unable to borrow at affordable rates.

Under Current Law, Federal Debt Will Stay at Historically High Levels Relative to GDP

The federal budget deficit, which shrank as a percentage of GDP for the third year in a row in 2012, will fall again in 2013, if current laws remain the same. At an estimated $845 billion, the 2013 imbalance would be the first deficit in five years below $1 trillion; and at 5.3 percent of GDP, it would be only about half as large, relative to the size of the economy, as the deficit was in 2009. Nevertheless, if the laws that govern taxes and spending do not change, federal debt held by the public will reach 76 percent of GDP by the end of this fiscal year, the largest percentage since 1950. With revenues expected to rise more rapidly than spending in the next few years under current law, the deficit is projected to dip as low as 2.4 percent of GDP by 2015 (see Summary Table 1). In later years, however, projected deficits rise steadily, reaching almost 4 percent of GDP in 2023. For the 2014–2023 period, deficits in CBO's baseline projections total $7.0 trillion. With such deficits, federal debt would remain above 73 percent of GDP— far higher than the 39 percent average seen over the past four decades. (As recently as the end of 2007, federal debt equaled just 36 percent of GDP.) Moreover, debt would be increasing relative to the size of the economy in the second half of the decade. Those projections are not CBO's predictions of future outcomes. As specified in law, CBO's baseline projections are constructed under the assumption that current laws generally remain unchanged, so that they can serve as a benchmark against which potential changes in law can be measured.

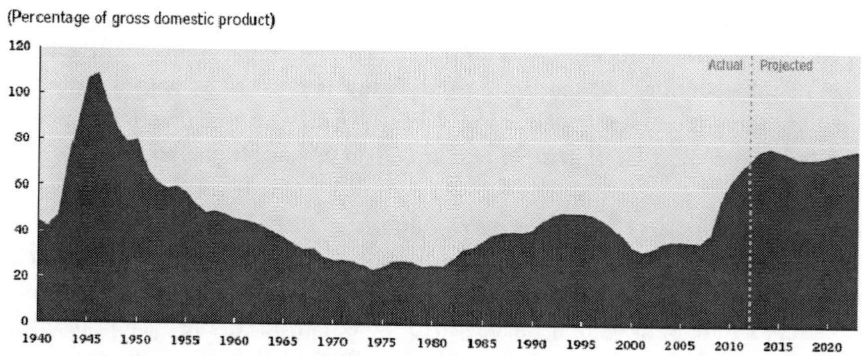

Source: Congressional Budget Office.

Summary Figure 1. Federal Debt Held by the Public.

Revenues

Federal revenues will increase by roughly 25 percent between 2013 and 2015 under current law, CBO projects. That increase is expected to result from a rise in income because of the growing economy, from policy changes that are scheduled to take effect during that period, and from policy changes that have already taken effect but whose full impact on revenues will not be felt until after this year (such as the recent increase in tax rates on income above certain thresholds). As a result of those factors, revenues are projected to grow from 15.8 percent of GDP in 2012 to 19.1 percent of GDP in 2015—compared with an average of 17.9 percent of GDP over the past 40 years. Under current law, revenues will remain at roughly 19 percent of GDP from 2015 through 2023, CBO estimates.

Outlays

In CBO's baseline projections, federal spending rises over the next few years in dollar terms but falls relative to the size of the economy. During those years, the growth of spending will be restrained both by the strengthening economy (as spending for programs such as unemployment compensation drops) and by provisions of the Budget Control Act of 2011 (Public Law 112-25). Although outlays are projected to decline from 22.8 percent of GDP in 2012 to 21.5 percent by 2017, they will still exceed their 40-year average of 21.0 percent. (Outlays peaked at 25.2 percent of GDP in 2009 but have fallen relative to GDP in the past few years.) After 2017, if current laws remain in place, outlays will start growing again as a percentage of GDP. The aging of the population, increasing health care costs, and a significant expansion of eligibility for federal subsidies for health insurance will substantially boost spending for Social Security and for major health care programs relative to the size of the economy. At the same time, rising interest rates will significantly increase the government's debt-service costs. In CBO's baseline, outlays reach about 23 percent of GDP in 2023 and are on an upward trajectory.

Changes from CBO's Previous Projections

The deficits projected in CBO's current baseline are significantly larger than the ones in CBO's baseline of August 2012. At that time, CBO projected deficits totaling $2.3 trillion for the 2013–2022 period; in the current baseline, the total deficit for that period has risen by $4.6 trillion. That increase stems chiefly from the enactment of the American Taxpayer Relief Act of 2012 (P.L. 112-240), which made changes to tax and spending laws that will boost deficits by a total of $4.0 trillion (excluding debt-service costs) between 2013 and 2022, according to estimates by CBO and the staff of the Joint Committee on Taxation. CBO's updated baseline also takes into account other legislative actions since August, as well as a new economic forecast and some technical revisions to its projections.

Looming Policy Decisions May Have a Substantial Effect on the Budget Outlook

Current law leaves many key budget issues unresolved, and this year, lawmakers will face three significant budgetary deadlines:

- Automatic reductions in spending are scheduled to be implemented at the beginning of March; when that happens, funding for many government activities will be reduced by 5 percent or more.
- The continuing resolution that currently provides operational funding for much of the government will expire in late March. If no additional appropriations are provided by then, nonessential functions of the government will have to cease operations.
- A statutory limit on federal debt, which was temporarily removed, will take effect again in mid-May. The Treasury will be able to continue borrowing for a short time after that by using what are known as extraordinary measures. But to avoid a default on the government's obligations, the debt limit will need to be adjusted before those measures are exhausted later in the year.

Budgetary outcomes will also be affected by decisions about whether to continue certain policies that have been in effect in recent years. Such policies could be continued, for example, by extending some tax provisions that are scheduled to expire (and that have routinely been extended in the past) or by preventing the 25 percent cut in Medicare's payment rates for physicians that is due to occur in 2014. If, for instance, lawmakers eliminated the automatic spending cuts scheduled to take effect in March (but left in place the original caps on discretionary funding set by the Budget Control Act), prevented the sharp reduction in Medicare's payment rates for physicians, and extended the tax provisions that are scheduled to expire at the end of calendar year 2013 (or, in some cases, in later years), budget deficits would be substantially larger over the coming decade than in CBO's baseline projections.

Summary Table 1. CBO's Baseline Budget Projections

												Total	
	Actual, 2012	2013	2014	2015	2016	2017	2018	2019	2020	2021	2022	2023	2014- 2018	2014-2023
	In Billions of Dollars													
Revenues	2,449	2,708	3,003	3,373	3,591	3,765	3,937	4,101	4,279	4,496	4,734	4,961	17,669	40,241
Outlays	3,538	3,553	3,618	3,803	4,067	4,300	4,542	4,811	5,078	5,350	5,691	5,939	20,330	47,199
Deficit (-) or Surplus	-1,089	-845	-616	-430	-476	-535	-605	-710	-798	-854	-957	-978	-2,661	-6,958
On-budget	-1,151	-872	-630	-433	-476	-533	-598	-693	-763	-799	-878	-872	-2,670	-6,675
Off-budget[a]	62	27	14	3	*	-2	-6	-17	-35	-55	-79	-106	9	-283
Debt Held by the Public at the End of the Year	11,280	12,229	12,937	13,462	14,025	14,642	15,316	16,092	16,957	17,876	18,902	19,944	n.a.	n.a.
	As a Percentage of Gross Domestic Product													
Revenues	15.8	16.9	18.0	19.1	19.1	18.9	18.8	18.7	18.7	18.9	19.0	19.1	18.8	18.9
Outlays	22.8	22.2	21.7	21.6	21.6	21.5	21.7	22.0	22.2	22.4	22.9	22.9	21.6	22.1
Deficit	-7.0	-5.3	-3.7	-2.4	-2.5	-2.7	-2.9	-3.2	-3.5	-3.6	-3.8	-3.8	-2.8	-3.3
Debt Held by the Public														
at the End of the Year	72.5	76.3	77.7	76.3	74.6	73.4	73.1	73.5	74.2	75.0	76.0	77.0	n.a.	n.a.

Source: Congressional Budget Office.

Note: * = between -$500 million and zero; n.a. = not applicable.

a. Off-budget surpluses or deficits comprise surpluses or deficits in the Social Security trust funds and the net cash flow of the Postal Service.

With those changes, and no offsetting reductions in deficits, debt held by the public would rise to 87 percent of GDP by the end of 2023 rather than to 77 percent.

In addition to those decisions, lawmakers will continue to face the longer-term budgetary issues posed by the substantial federal debt and by the implications of rising health care costs and the aging of the population.

Economic Growth Is Likely to Be Slow in 2013 and Pick up in Later Years

The U.S. economy expanded modestly in calendar year 2012, continuing the slow recovery seen since the recession ended in mid-2009. Although economic growth is expected to remain slow again this year, CBO anticipates that underlying factors in the economy will spur a more rapid expansion beginning next year.

Even so, under the fiscal policies embodied in current law, output is expected to remain below its potential (or maximum sustainable) level until 2017. By CBO's estimates, in the fourth quarter of 2012, real (inflation-adjusted) GDP was about 51/2 percent below its potential level. That gap was only modestly smaller than the gap between actual and potential GDP that existed at the end of the recession (see Summary Figure 2) because the growth of output since then has been only slightly greater than the growth of potential output. With such a large gap between actual and potential GDP persisting for so long, CBO projects that the total loss of output, relative to the economy's potential, between 2007 and 2017 will be equivalent to nearly half of the output that the United States produced last year.

The Economic Outlook for 2013

CBO expects that economic activity will expand slowly this year, with real GDP growing by just 1.4 percent (see Summary Table 2). That slow growth reflects a combination of ongoing improvement in underlying economic factors and fiscal tightening that has already begun or is scheduled to occur—including the expiration of a 2 percentage-point cut in the Social Security payroll tax, an increase in tax rates on income above certain thresholds, and scheduled automatic reductions in federal spending. That subdued economic growth will limit businesses' need to hire additional workers, thereby causing the unemployment rate to stay near 8 percent this year, CBO projects. The rate of inflation and interest rates are projected to remain low.

The Economic Outlook for 2014 to 2018

After the economy adjusts this year to the fiscal tightening inherent in current law, underlying economic factors will lead to more rapid growth, CBO projects—3.4 percent in 2014 and an average of 3.6 percent a year from 2015 through 2018.

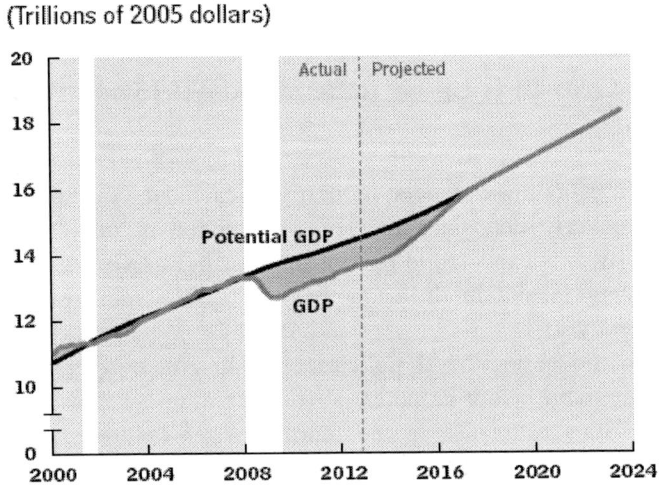

Sources: Congressional Budget Office; Department of Commerce, Bureau of Economic Analysis.

Notes: Potential gross domestic product (GDP) is CBO's estimate of the maximum sustainable level of output of the economy.

Data are quarterly. Actual data are plotted through the third quarter of 2012. Projections are plotted through the fourth quarter of 2023.

Summary Figure 2. GDP and Potential GDP.

In particular, CBO expects that the effects of the housing and financial crisis will continue to fade and that an upswing in housing construction (though from a very low level), rising real estate and stock prices, and increasing availability of credit will help to spur a virtuous cycle of faster growth in employment, income, consumer spending, and business investment over the next few years.

Nevertheless, under current law, CBO expects the unemployment rate to remain high—above 71/2 percent through 2014—before falling to 51/2 percent at the end of 2017. The rate of inflation is projected to rise slowly after this year: CBO estimates that the annual increase in the price index for personal consumption expenditures will reach about 2 percent in 2015.

The interest rate on 3-month Treasury bills—which has hovered near zero for the past several years—is expected to climb to 4 percent by the end of 2017, and the rate on 10-year Treasury notes is projected to rise from 2.1 percent in 2013 to 5.2 percent in 2017.

Summary Table 2. CBO's Economic Projections for Calendar Years 2012 to 2023

	Estimated, 2012	Forecast		Projected Annual Average	
		2013	2014	2015–2018	2019–2023
	Fourth Quarter to Fourth Quarter (Percentage change)				
Real Gross Domestic Product	1.9	1.4	3.4	3.6	2.2
Inflation					
PCE price index	1.5	1.3	1.8	1.9	2.0
Core PCE price index[a]	1.5	1.5	1.9	2.0	2.0
Consumer price index[b]	1.9 [c]	1.5	2.0	2.2	2.3
Core consumer price index[a]	1.9 [c]	1.8	2.0	2.2	2.3
	Fourth Quarter Level (Percent)				
Unemployment Rate	7.8 [c]	8.0	7.6	5.5 [d]	5.2 [e]
	Calendar Year Average (Percent)				
Interest Rates					
Three-month Treasury bills	0.1 [c]	0.1	0.2	2.2	4.0
Ten-year Treasury notes	1.8 [c]	2.1	2.7	4.5	5.2

Source: Congressional Budget Office. (Actual values for 2012 are from Department of Labor, Bureau of Labor Statistics; Federal Reserve.) Notes: Economic projections for each year from 2012 to 2023 appear in Appendix B.

The numbers shown here do not reflect the values for GDP and related series released by the Commerce Department's Bureau of Economic Analysis on January 30.

PCE = personal consumption expenditures.

[a] Excludes prices for food and energy.

[b] The consumer price index for all urban consumers.

[c] Actual value for 2012.

[d] Value for 2018.

[e] Value for 2023.

The Economic Outlook for 2019 to 2023

For the second half of the coming decade, CBO does not attempt to predict the cyclical ups and downs of the economy; rather, CBO assumes that GDP will stay at its maximum sustainable level. On that basis, CBO projects that both actual and potential real GDP will grow at an average rate of 21/4 percent a year between 2019 and 2023. That pace is much slower than the average growth rate of potential GDP since 1950. The main reason is that the growth of the labor force will slow down because of the retirement of the baby boomers and an end to the long-standing increase in women's participation in the labor force. CBO also projects that the unemployment rate will fall to 5.2 percent by 2023 and that inflation and interest rates will stay at about their 2018 levels throughout the 2019–2023 period.

SECTION 1. THE BUDGET OUTLOOK

If current laws remain in place, the Congressional Budget Office (CBO) estimates, the federal budget deficit will total $845 billion in fiscal year 2013; this will be the first time since 2008 that the budget shortfall will be less than $1 trillion. At 5.3 percent of gross domestic product (GDP), that deficit will be well below the peak of 10.1 percent in 2009 but still larger than in all but one year between 1947 and 2008 (see Figure 1-1). As a result, debt held by the public is estimated to increase to 76 percent of GDP by the end of 2013, the largest ratio since 1950.

CBO constructs its baseline projections of federal revenues and spending under the assumption that current laws generally remain unchanged. Under that assumption, revenues are projected to rise as a share of GDP over the next few years—from nearly 16 percent in 2012 to 17 percent in 2013, 18 percent in 2014, and then about 19 percent from 2015 through 2023 (see Table 1-1). Outlays in the baseline drop from almost 23 percent of GDP in 2012 to 21.5 percent in 2017; they begin to rise again later in the decade, reaching 22.9 percent in 2023. As a result, in CBO's baseline projections, annual deficits remain above their prerecession 40-year average (1968 to 2007) through 2023 relative to the size of the economy. They decline as a percentage of GDP for the next two years, to 3.7 percent in 2014 and 2.4 percent in 2015. But, beginning in 2016, deficits in the baseline start to increase again, reaching 3.8 percent of GDP at the end of the 10-year projection period. Those accumulating deficits would boost debt held by the public to a peak of almost 78 percent of GDP by the end of 2014, CBO estimates. Relative to the nation's output, the debt would decline over the following few years but then start to climb again in the latter part of the projection period, reaching 77 percent of GDP at the end of 2023. (As recently as the end of 2007, the debt was equal to only 36 percent of GDP.) Although relative stability in the debt as a share of GDP over the next 10 years would be a welcome development after its sharp upward surge during the past several years, the projected path of the federal budget remains a significant concern for several reasons. First, under the current-law baseline, the projected debt is very high by historical standards. Throughout the 2013– 2023 period, debt held by the public is projected to be significantly greater relative to GDP than at any time since just after World War II; at no time is it anticipated to fall below the percentage of GDP it represented in any year between 1951 and 2012. If the amount of debt held by the public remains so large, federal spending on interest payments will increase substantially when interest rates rise to more normal levels. Because federal borrowing generally reduces national saving, the stock of capital assets, such as equipment and structures, will be smaller and aggregate wages will be less than if the debt were lower. In addition, lawmakers will have less flexibility than they ordinarily might to use tax and spending policies to respond to unanticipated challenges. Moreover, such a large debt poses an increased risk of precipitating a fiscal crisis, during which investors would lose so much confidence in the government's ability to manage its budget that the government would be unable to borrow at affordable rates.[1] Second, deficits and the debt would be even larger if current laws were modified, as they have been in the past, to delay or undo certain scheduled changes in policy. CBO's baseline projections incorporate the assumption that the automatic spending reductions established by the Budget Control Act of 2011 (Public Law 112-25) will take effect at the beginning of March, that sharp reductions in Medicare's payment rates for physicians' services will occur at the beginning of January 2014, and that certain tax provisions that have regularly been extended but are set to expire at the end of the calendar year (or, in some cases, in later years) will expire as scheduled. If those provisions of current law were removed, and if other changes in policies with offsetting effects on budget deficits were not enacted, budget deficits during the coming decade would be substantially larger than those shown in CBO's baseline projections. Specifically, under an alternative fiscal scenario, if those provisions of law were undone, debt held by the public would reach 87 percent of GDP at the end of 2023. Third, deficits and the debt also might be larger than in CBO's baseline projections because holding discretionary spending within the limits required under current law might be difficult. Even if automatic spending reductions from the

Budget Control Act were avoided, the original caps on discretionary budget authority established by that legislation would reduce such spending to an unusually small amount relative to the size of the economy. CBO projects that, with just those original caps in place, discretionary spending would equal 5.8 percent of GDP in 2023; by comparison, the lowest share for discretionary spending in any year since 1962 (the earliest year for which such data have been reported) was 6.2 percent in 1999. (Overall federal spending would be a larger share of GDP than its average during the past 40 years because of increased spending on Social Security, Medicare, Medicaid, health care subsidies for low-income people, and interest payments on the debt.) Because the allocation of discretionary spending is determined by annual appropriation acts, lawmakers have not yet decided which specific government services and benefits will be reduced or constrained to meet the specified limits.

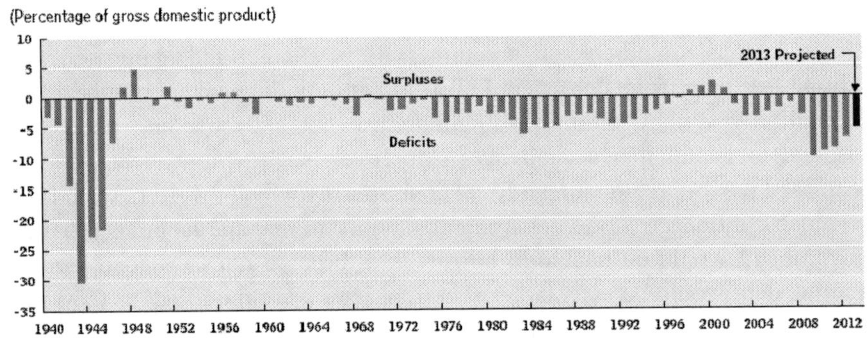

Source: Congressional Budget Office.

Figure 1-1. Total Deficits or Surpluses.

Fourth, projections for the period covered in this report do not fully reflect long-term budgetary pressures, although upward pressure on the federal debt is evident in the later years of that period. Under current law, the aging of the population, the rising costs of health care, and the scheduled expansion in federal subsidies for health insurance will substantially boost federal spending on Social Security and the government's major health care programs, relative to GDP, for the next 10 years and for decades thereafter. Unless the laws governing those programs are changed—or the increased spending is accompanied by corresponding reductions in other spending, sufficiently higher tax revenues, or a combination of the two—debt will rise sharply relative to GDP after 2023.[2]

Table 1-1. CBO's Baseline Budget Projections

	Actual, 2012	2013	2014	2015	2016	2017	2018	2019	2020	2021	2022	2023	Total 2014-2018	Total 2014-2023
						In Billions of Dollars								
Revenues														
Individual income taxes	1,132	1,264	1,355	1,540	1,674	1,810	1,929	2,040	2,158	2,282	2,412	2,548	8,308	19,747
Social insurance taxes	845	953	1,021	1,068	1,129	1,195	1,256	1,314	1,372	1,433	1,498	1,565	5,670	12,852
Corporate income taxes	242	251	356	448	489	511	512	498	492	493	499	506	2,317	4,805
Other	229	241	270	317	299	249	239	249	258	288	326	342	1,374	2,837
Total	2,449	2,708	3,003	3,373	3,591	3,765	3,937	4,101	4,279	4,496	4,734	4,961	17,669	40,241
On-budget	1,880	2,038	2,271	2,607	2,779	2,904	3,029	3,149	3,285	3,457	3,651	3,832	13,589	30,963
Off-budget[a]	570	670	732	766	812	862	908	952	995	1,039	1,084	1,129	4,080	9,278
Outlays														
Mandatory	2,031	2,116	2,205	2,342	2,535	2,655	2,768	2,924	3,087	3,263	3,501	3,658	12,504	28,938
Discretionary	1,285	1,213	1,170	1,189	1,209	1,233	1,257	1,293	1,324	1,356	1,396	1,424	6,059	12,852
Net interest	223	224	243	272	323	412	517	593	667	730	795	857	1,767	5,410
Total	3,538	3,553	3,618	3,803	4,067	4,300	4,542	4,811	5,078	5,350	5,691	5,939	20,330	47,199
On-budget	3,031	2,910	2,901	3,039	3,255	3,437	3,627	3,842	4,048	4,256	4,529	4,704	16,259	37,637
Off-budget[a]	508	643	717	763	812	864	915	969	1,030	1,094	1,162	1,235	4,071	9,562
Deficit (-) or Surplus	-1,089	-845	-616	-430	-476	-535	-605	-710	-798	-854	-957	-978	-2,661	-6,958
On-budget	-1,151	-872	-630	-433	-476	-533	-598	-693	-763	-799	-878	-872	-2,670	-6,675
Off-budget[a]	62	27	14	3	*	-2	-6	-17	-35	-55	-79	-106	9	-283
Debt Held by the Public	11,280	12,229	12,937	13,462	14,025	14,642	15,316	16,092	16,957	17,876	18,902	19,944	n.a.	n.a.
Memorandum:														
Gross Domestic Product	15,549	16,034	16,646	17,632	18,792	19,959	20,943	21,890	22,854	23,842	24,858	25,910	93,972	213,326
					As a Percentage of Gross Domestic Product									
Revenues														
Individual income taxes	7.3	7.9	8.1	8.7	8.9	9.1	9.2	9.3	9.4	9.6	9.7	9.8	8.8	9.3
Social insurance taxes	5.4	5.9	6.1	6.1	6.0	6.0	6.0	6.0	6.0	6.0	6.0	6.0	6.0	6.0

Table 1-1. (Continued)

	Actual, 2012	2013	2014	2015	2016	2017	2018	2019	2020	2021	2022	2023	Total 2014-2018	Total 2014-2023
						In Billions of Dollars								
Corporate income taxes	1.6	1.6	2.1	2.5	2.6	2.6	2.4	2.3	2.2	2.1	2.0	2.0	2.5	2.3
Other	1.5	1.5	1.6	1.8	1.6	1.2	1.1	1.1	1.1	1.2	1.3	1.3	1.5	1.3
Total	15.8	16.9	18.0	19.1	19.1	18.9	18.8	18.7	18.7	18.9	19.0	19.1	18.8	18.9
On-budget	12.1	12.7	13.6	14.8	14.8	14.5	14.5	14.4	14.4	14.5	14.7	14.8	14.5	14.5
Off-budget[a]	3.7	4.2	4.4	4.3	4.3	4.3	4.3	4.3	4.4	4.4	4.4	4.4	4.3	4.3
Outlays														
Mandatory	13.1	13.2	13.2	13.3	13.5	13.3	13.2	13.4	13.5	13.7	14.1	14.1	13.3	13.6
Discretionary	8.3	7.6	7.0	6.7	6.4	6.2	6.0	5.9	5.8	5.7	5.6	5.5	6.4	6.0
Net interest	1.4	1.4	1.5	1.5	1.7	2.1	2.5	2.7	2.9	3.1	3.2	3.3	1.9	2.5
Total	22.8	22.2	21.7	21.6	21.6	21.5	21.7	22.0	22.2	22.4	22.9	22.9	21.6	22.1
On-budget	19.5	18.2	17.4	17.2	17.3	17.2	17.3	17.6	17.7	17.8	18.2	18.2	17.3	17.6
Off-budget[a]	3.3	4.0	4.3	4.3	4.3	4.3	4.4	4.4	4.5	4.6	4.7	4.8	4.3	4.5
Deficit (-) or Surplus	-7.0	-5.3	-3.7	-2.4	-2.5	-2.7	-2.9	-3.2	-3.5	-3.6	-3.8	-3.8	-2.8	-3.3
On-budget	-7.4	-5.4	-3.8	-2.5	-2.5	-2.7	-2.9	-3.2	-3.3	-3.3	-3.5	-3.4	-2.8	-3.1
Off-budget[a]	0.4	0.2	0.1	**	**	**	**	-0.1	-0.2	-0.2	-0.3	-0.4	**	-0.1
Debt Held by the Public	72.5	76.3	77.7	76.3	74.6	73.4	73.1	73.5	74.2	75.0	76.0	77.0	n.a.	n.a.

Source: Congressional Budget Office.

Note: * = between -$500 million and zero; n.a. = not applicable; ** = between -0.05 percent and 0.05 percent.

a. The revenues and outlays of the Social Security trust funds and the net cash flow of the Postal Service are classified as off-budget.

Deciding now what policy changes to make to resolve that long-term imbalance would allow for gradual implementation, which would give households, businesses, and state and local governments time to plan and adjust their behavior. The baseline budget outlook has changed substantially from the projections that CBO published in August 2012.[3] At that time, deficits projected under current law totaled $2.3 trillion for the 2013–2022 period, or 1.1 percent of GDP. They are now $4.6 trillion larger.

The majority of the increase in projected deficits stems from enactment of the American Taxpayer Relief Act of 2012 (P.L. 112-240) (see Box 1-1). Most of that effect results from reductions in revenues stemming from three types of changes:

- The permanent extension of lower tax rates for income below certain thresholds and other tax provisions originally enacted in 2001 and 2003,
- The permanent limit on the reach of the alternative minimum tax (AMT), and
- The temporary extension of other tax provisions that had expired at the end of 2011 or 2012.

The projections that make up CBO's baseline are not intended to be a forecast of budgetary outcomes. Rather, they are meant to provide a neutral benchmark that policymakers can use to assess the potential effects of policy decisions. Although CBO's baseline does not incorporate potential changes in law, this section shows how some alternatives would affect the budget over the next 10 years.

For example, under CBO's baseline, funding for overseas contingency operations—that is, military operations and related activities in Afghanistan or other countries—is assumed to continue throughout the projection period at the level provided for 2013, with adjustments for inflation. Such funding has declined in recent years, however, so CBO has constructed a policy alternative reflecting that trend.

Under that scenario, war-related funding would continue declining through 2015, rather than growing at the rate of inflation.

As a result, the total deficit for the 2014–2023 period would be about $600 billion below the amounts projected in the baseline. In the other direction, if the automatic spending reductions put in place by the Budget Control Act did not take effect, deficits would be about $1 trillion higher over the projection period. (For more details, see "Alternative Assumptions About Fiscal Policy.")

Key Budgetary Decisions Facing Lawmakers in 2013

By changing some income tax rates and making permanent changes to the AMT, among other things, the American Taxpayer Relief Act has reduced the uncertainty surrounding federal fiscal policy. Nevertheless, many key budget issues remain unresolved.

Over the next few months, lawmakers will face three significant budgetary deadlines:

- Automatic spending reductions scheduled to be implemented at the beginning of March;
- The expiration in late March of a continuing resolution that provides operational funding for much of the federal government; and
- The statutory limit on federal debt, temporarily removed, which takes effect again in mid-May.

In addition, lawmakers still face the longer-term budget issues posed by the large current and projected federal debt and the implications of rising health care costs and the aging population.

Automatic Spending Reductions

The provisions of the Budget Control Act that established automatic procedures to restrain discretionary and mandatory spending are set to take effect on March 1; if fully implemented, they will reduce total funding in 2013 by $85 billion. (The American Taxpayer Relief Act delayed the reduction by two months and reduced it by $24 billion.) CBO estimates that, in 2013, discretionary funding (which is provided through annual appropriations) will decline by $71 billion and funding for mandatory programs (which is not subject to annual appropriations) will be reduced by $14 billion, as a result of those procedures. By CBO's estimate, budgetary resources for defense (other than spending for military personnel) will be cut by around 8 percent across the board, and nondefense funding that is subject to the automatic reductions will be cut by between 5 percent and 6 percent (see Table 1-2 on page 14).[4] According to that estimate, discretionary outlays will drop by $35 billion and mandatory spending will be reduced by $9 billion this year as a direct result of those procedures; additional reductions in outlays attributable to the cuts in 2013 funding will occur in later years.[5] The deficit for 2013 will depend in part on whether those cuts are allowed to take place, are canceled (in whole or in part), or are replaced with other measures designed to reduce the deficit.

Continuing Resolution

Federal agencies are now operating under the Continuing Appropriations Resolution, 2013 (P.L. 112-175), which set discretionary funding for 2013 at an annual rate of $1.047 trillion, the sum of the caps established by the Budget Control Act (before the American Taxpayer Relief Act reduced the caps by $4 billion). That funding will expire on March 27, although following the rules in the Balanced Budget and Emergency Deficit Control Act of 1985, CBO's baseline incorporates the assumption that such funding will be extended at the current amount for the remainder of the fiscal year. If no additional appropriations are provided, nonessential functions of the government will cease operations after March 27. If final appropriations differ from those provided in the continuing resolution, CBO's projections of discretionary outlays will be affected for 2013 and future years.

Statutory Limit on Federal Debt

Until recently, the amount of debt that the Department of the Treasury could issue to the public and to other government accounts was capped at $16.394 trillion; that limit was reached at the end of December 2012. At that time, the Treasury began using what are known as extraordinary measures for managing cash and borrowing in order to continue funding the operations of the federal government. Lawmakers have recently suspended the limitation on borrowing through May 18, 2013, and on May 19, the existing debt limit will be raised by the amount of borrowing that occurred while the limitation was suspended (that is, from early February to May 18). If no further action is taken before May 19, the Treasury will once again resort to extraordinary measures to allow the government to continue operating normally. To avoid defaulting on the federal government's obligations, including possibly defaulting on the government's debt obligations, the debt ceiling will need to be adjusted before those extraordinary measures are exhausted later in the year.

Budgetary Outcomes in 2012 and the Outlook for 2013

In fiscal year 2012, the budget deficit totaled $1.1 trillion—$206 billion less than the shortfall recorded in 2011. As a percentage of GDP, the deficit declined from 8.7 percent in 2011 to 7.0 percent in 2012. Under current law, the budget shortfall will decline again in 2013, to $845 billion, or 5.3 percent of GDP, CBO estimates.

Revenues

Federal revenues increased by $147 billion (or 6 percent) in 2012, and they are projected to grow by $259 billion (or 11 percent) in 2013. If current laws remain the same, CBO estimates, revenues in 2013 will equal $2.7 trillion, or 16.9 percent of GDP, higher than the 15.8 percent of GDP recorded in 2012 and the highest percentage since 2008, although still below the average of about 18 percent of GDP over the past 40 years. The increase in revenues as a share of GDP expected for 2013 results largely from increases in payroll tax rates for all workers and individual income tax rates for upper incomes. In 2012, receipts from corporate income taxes accounted for a large part of the increase in total revenues, rising by $61 billion (or 34 percent). Most of the gain resulted from changes in tax rules, notably a reduction between 2011 and 2012 in the portion of investments in equipment that businesses could deduct from their taxes in the year those investments were made. Receipts from individual income taxes rose by $41 billion (or 4 percent), and receipts from social insurance taxes rose by $27 billion (or 3 percent). Much of those gains resulted from increases in wages and salaries, which grew by about 3 percent last year. Receipts from other sources increased by $18 billion, mainly because of higher collections of estate and gift taxes and excise taxes. The American Taxpayer Relief Act of 2012 (Public Law 112-240), which was enacted in early January 2013, permanently extended some lower tax rates and other tax provisions that expired at the end of calendar year 2012, modified the alternative minimum tax (AMT) to permanently limit its reach, and temporarily extended other tax provisions. The law also extended emergency unemployment benefits, made changes in several health care programs, temporarily forestalled some provisions of the Budget Control Act of 2011 (P.L. 112-25), and extended agricultural subsidies.[1] The Congressional Budget Office (CBO) and the staff of the Joint Committee on Taxation (JCT) estimate that, relative to laws in place at the end of 2012, enactment of the American Taxpayer Relief Act will add $4.0 trillion to federal deficits over the 2013–2022 period (see the table). Almost all of that amount—$3.9 trillion—will result from the extension of tax provisions. Other changes will increase deficits through 2022 by $42 billion. Major provisions of the law are discussed below.

Extensions of Tax Provisions

With some modifications that affect high-income taxpayers, the new law made permanent several tax provisions originally enacted in 2001 and 2003 that expired on December 31, 2012, including the following:

- Lower tax rates on ordinary income;
- An expanded 15 percent tax bracket and an increase in the standard deduction for married couples;
- The child tax credit of $1,000 per child;
- The 15 percent tax rate on long-term capital gains realizations and dividends; and
- The estate and gift tax rules in effect in 2012, with modifications.

At the end of 2012, tax rates on ordinary income were to rise from the lower rates in effect that year (10, 15, 25, 28, 33, and 35 percent) to the rates that had been in effect before 2001 (15, 28, 31, 36, and 39.6 percent). The new law permanently extended the lower rates, with the following exception: For single taxpayers whose income is above $400,000 and for married taxpayers filing jointly whose income is above $450,000, the new law sets the top tax rate at 39.6 percent, the same top rate that had been scheduled to take effect before the law was enacted. The law permanently extended the increase in the child tax credit from $500 to $1,000 per child and provisions (also enacted in 2001) that made the credit refundable for more families. Before 2001, the credit was refundable only for families with three or more children. It also extended, through 2017, a lower earned income threshold for the refundability of the child tax credit, expansions to the earned income credit, and the American Opportunity Tax Credit— a refundable credit for postsecondary education expenses—all enacted in 2009.

Box 1-1. The American Taxpayer Relief Act of 2012

The American Taxpayer Relief Act of 2012 (Public Law 112-240), which was enacted in early January 2013, permanently extended some lower tax rates and other tax provisions that expired at the end of calendar year 2012, modified the alternative minimum tax (AMT) to permanently limit its reach, and temporarily extended other tax provisions. The law also extended emergency unemployment benefits, made changes in several health care programs, temporarily forestalled some provisions of the Budget Control Act of 2011 (P.L. 112-25), and extended agricultural subsidies.[1] The Congressional Budget Office (CBO) and the staff of the Joint Committee on Taxation (JCT) estimate that, relative to laws in place at the end of 2012, enactment of the American Taxpayer Relief Act will add $4.0 trillion to federal deficits over the 2013–2022 period (see the table).

Almost all of that amount—$3.9 trillion—will result from the extension of tax provisions.

Other changes will increase deficits through 2022 by $42 billion. Major provisions of the law are discussed below.

Extensions of Tax Provisions

With some modifications that affect high-income taxpayers, the new law made permanent several tax provisions originally enacted in 2001 and 2003 that expired on December 31, 2012, including the following:

- Lower tax rates on ordinary income;
- An expanded 15 percent tax bracket and an increase in the standard deduction for married couples;
- The child tax credit of $1,000 per child;
- The 15 percent tax rate on long-term capital gains realizations and dividends; and
- The estate and gift tax rules in effect in 2012, with modifications.

At the end of 2012, tax rates on ordinary income were to rise from the lower rates in effect that year (10, 15, 25, 28, 33, and 35 percent) to the rates that had been in effect before 2001 (15, 28, 31, 36, and 39.6 percent). The new law permanently extended the lower rates, with the following exception:

For single taxpayers whose income is above $400,000 and for married taxpayers filing jointly whose income is above $450,000, the new law sets the top tax rate at 39.6 percent, the same top rate that had been scheduled to take effect before the law was enacted. The law permanently extended the increase in the child tax credit from $500 to $1,000 per child and provisions (also enacted in 2001) that made the credit refundable for more families.

Before 2001, the credit was refundable only for families with three or more children. It also extended, through 2017, a lower earned income threshold for the refundability of the child tax credit, expansions to the earned income credit, and the American Opportunity Tax Credit— a refundable credit for postsecondary education expenses—all enacted in 2009. Under prior law, the tax rate on capital gains was scheduled to rise to 20 percent and the tax rate on dividends was scheduled to equal the taxpayer's rate on other income.

The new law kept the 15 percent limit on those rates for most taxpayers and raised the top rate on dividends and capital gains to 20 percent for high-income taxpayers. Separately, the law permanently extended the estate and gift tax rules in effect in 2012, although with a higher top tax rate of 40 percent. The law also increased the AMT's exemption amount (the higher amount had expired at the end of 2011) and indexed that amount (and other parameters of the tax) for inflation, beginning in 2013. Several tax provisions extended by the new law through calendar year 2013 had expired at the end of calendar year 2011. Some of those, including the research and experimentation tax credit, have routinely been extended in the past. The law also extended for one year a tax provision that allows businesses to immediately deduct 50 percent of new investments in equipment.

Effects on the Deficit of the American Taxpayer Relief Act of 2012
(Billions of dollars)

											Total	
	2013	2014	2015	2016	2017	2018	2019	2020	2021	2022	2013-2017	2013-2022
Extensions of Tax Provisions	-280	-336	-313	-344	-375	-406	-417	-450	-485	-521	-1,648	-3,928
Unemployment Compensation	-22	-8	*	*	*	*	*	*	0	0	-30	-30
Medicare and Other Health Care Programs[a]	-13	-5	3	3	3	*	*	1	1	5	-8	-1
Other Provisions	-14	-5	-1	*	1	1	2	2	2	2	-20	-12
Total Change in the Deficit	-329	-354	-311	-340	-371	-405	-416	-448	-482	-514	-1,706	-3,970

Source: Congressional Budget Office.

Notes: Negative numbers indicate an increase in the deficit; positive numbers indicate a decrease in the deficit.

* = between -$500 million and zero.

a. The estimate shown in this table corrects an error in CBO's original cost estimate for the legislation, which showed a net cost of $1.7 billion, instead of the $1 billion net cost shown here, over the 2013–2022 period in the line labeled "Subtotal, Title VI, Estimated Outlays." See Congressional Budget Office, cost estimate for H.R. 8, the American Taxpayer Relief Act of 2012 (as passed by the Senate on January 1, 2013), www.cbo.gov /publication/43829.

Changes to Other Provisions

The new law extended emergency unemployment compensation for a year, allowing certain people who have been unemployed for a long time to receive benefits through December 2013.

That provision had an estimated cost of $30 billion.

The law prevented Medicare's payments to physicians from being cut by about 27 percent, as prior law would have required. Instead, through December 2013, payment rates will remain at amounts in effect in 2012. The law also postpones reductions in Medicare's payments for several other types of services, including ambulance services and speech, physical, and occupational therapy.

The estimated $30 billion cost of those provisions was mostly offset by other changes to Medicare and other federal health care programs. The largest offsetting savings come from reductions in Medicare's payment rates for inpatient hospital and dialysis services and from a reduction in Medicaid's payments to states for hospitals that serve a disproportionate share of Medicaid patients and patients who have no health insurance. The law also delayed and reduced the amount of the automatic spending reductions required by the Budget Control Act of 2011.

Those reductions are now scheduled to take effect on March 1, rather than on January 1, and the amount of the reductions in budget authority was reduced by $24 billion. In addition, the law permits individuals to convert balances in tax-deferred 401(k) and similar employment-based retirement accounts into Roth accounts. Such conversions will result in taxes being paid earlier than they otherwise would be, increasing revenues by $12 billion through 2022, JCT estimates, but reducing revenues beyond 2022. Taken together, those provisions will increase deficits by an estimated $12 billion over fiscal years 2013 through 2022.

[1]. The budgetary effects of the law's provisions to extend federal agriculture programs and to prohibit Members of Congress from receiving cost-of-living adjustments in 2013 are not included in estimates shown here, either because those effects were already reflected in CBO's baseline projections or because the savings had been credited to previous legislation.

In 2013, CBO expects that revenues will increase at a faster pace, mostly as a result of robust increases in receipts from individual income and social insurance taxes. Receipts from individual income taxes are anticipated to rise by $131 billion (or 12 percent). Just under half of the increase is from changes in tax provisions, including increases in income tax rates and a new surtax on investment income, both affecting certain high-income taxpayers, beginning in January 2013. In addition, shifting of income—such as capital gains realizations from stock and other asset sales, wages and salaries, and dividends—mainly from calendar year 2013 into late 2012 in anticipation of those rate changes (and in anticipation of possible rate changes that did not ultimately occur) is expected to increase revenues in fiscal year 2013 and reduce them in 2014, when some of the taxes on that income would have been paid.[6] The other, slightly larger part of the expected gain in 2013 stems from increases in wages and salaries, capital gains realizations (apart from the effects of the changing tax rates), and retirement and other types of income.

Table 1-2. CBO's Estimates of Automatic Spending Reductions for 2013

	Reduction in Budgetary Resources (Billions of dollars)	Percentage Reduction
Defense		
Discretionary	42.7	7.9
Mandatory	*	7.8
Total	42.7	7.9
Nondefense		
Discretionary	28.7	5.3
Mandatory		
Medicare spending subject to 2 percent limit[a]	9.9	2.0
Other	4.0	5.8
Total	42.7	4.6

Source: Congressional Budget Office.

Notes: Budgetary resources subject to sequestration include new budget authority, unobligated balances for defense programs, and direct spending authority.

These estimates use CBO's baseline projections for 2013 as a basis for allocating the reductions among categories. However, the Office of Management and Budget will make the official calculations, using its own numbers; as a result, the actual percentage reductions could differ from those shown here by a few tenths of a percentage point in either direction. * = between zero and $50 million.

a. The sequestration cannot exceed 2 percent for payments made for individual services covered under Medicare Part A (Hospital Insurance) and Part B (Medical Insurance) and monthly contractual payments for Part C (Medicare Advantage plans) and Part D (prescription drug benefit plans). According to the rules for sequestration, reductions in Medicare will begin in the month after the sequestration order is issued, thereby delaying some of the effect on outlays until the following fiscal year.

Receipts from social insurance taxes in 2013 are expected to increase by $108 billion (or 13 percent), mainly because of the expiration of the 2 percentage-point reduction in the employee's portion of the Social Security payroll tax rate that was in effect in calendar years 2011 and 2012.

Corporate income tax receipts are estimated to rise by $9 billion (or 4 percent) in 2013 because of an increase in the average tax rate on domestic economic profits (the profits themselves are anticipated to be about the same as in 2012).

Outlays

In 2012, federal spending dropped by $60 billion (or 1.7 percent) from its 2011 mark to an amount slightly above $3.5 trillion. However, that decline occurred in part because about $30 billion in payments that ordinarily would have been made on October 1, 2011 (which fell on a weekend), were shifted into September 2011 (and thus into the previous fiscal year). Had the shift not occurred, outlays in fiscal year 2012 would have been about the same as in fiscal year 2011. That result stands in marked contrast to most of the past decade; in 7 out of 10 years, federal outlays increased by more than 6 percent from the year before.

CBO estimates that outlays in 2013 will total $3.55 trillion, within 0.4 percent of outlays recorded in 2012. As a percentage of GDP, outlays will fall slightly, according to CBO's estimates, from 22.8 percent in 2012 to 22.2 percent—a share that is still larger than in any year between 1986 and 2008.

Mandatory Spending

Spending for mandatory programs changed little in 2012, increasing by just 0.5 percent, or $10 billion. Without the shift of about $27 billion in certain payments from 2012 into 2011, however, mandatory outlays would have risen by 3 percent, or $63 billion. (Mandatory outlays grew at an average annual rate of about 7 percent between 2002 and 2011.) Mandatory spending (adjusted for that shift of payments) is projected to increase by 3 percent again in 2013.

The Troubled Asset Relief Program

The largest change in mandatory spending in 2012 was for the Troubled Asset Relief Program (TARP). By law, the costs of investments made under that program are estimated as the present value of anticipated net outlays, calculated using a discount rate that incorporates market risk.[7] The estimates are adjusted annually to account for an updated valuation of the cash flows associated with the program.

In 2012, the estimated costs of the program's transactions made in earlier years were revised upward by $21 billion. In addition, the TARP recorded $3 billion in new spending, primarily for mortgage assistance, thus pushing outlays for the program to about $25 billion in 2012.

Table 1-3. Mandatory Outlays Projected in CBO's Baseline (Billions of dollars)

	Actual, 2012	2013	2014	2015	2016	2017	2018	2019	2020	2021	2022	2023	Total 2014-2018	Total 2014-2023
Social Security														
Old-Age and Survivors Insurance	632	668	706	747	792	841	894	951	1,013	1,075	1,140	1,209	3,979	9,368
Disability Insurance	136	142	148	155	161	167	173	179	186	195	204	214	804	1,781
Subtotal	768	810	854	902	953	1,008	1,067	1,130	1,199	1,270	1,344	1,423	4,783	11,149
Health Care Programs														
Medicare[a]	551	592	605	627	680	706	741	811	867	928	1,024	1,079	3,360	8,070
Medicaid	251	265	297	331	372	399	422	449	476	505	536	572	1,821	4,360
Health insurance subsidies, exchanges, and related spending	*	1	21	42	74	95	106	111	115	122	128	134	339	949
MERHCF	9	9	9	10	10	11	12	13	13	14	15	16	52	124
Children's Health Insurance Program	9	9	13	14	8	6	6	6	6	6	6	6	47	75
Other	6	8	6	25	23	29	26	28	30	32	35	38	109	272
Subtotal[a]	825	885	951	1,049	1,168	1,246	1,314	1,417	1,508	1,608	1,744	1,845	5,727	13,850
Income Security														
Supplemental Nutrition Assistance Program	80	82	80	79	79	78	76	75	74	73	73	73	392	760
Supplemental Security Income	47	53	55	56	63	59	56	63	64	66	74	70	289	626

Table 1-3. (Continued)

	Actual, 2012	2013	2014	2015	2016	2017	2018	2019	2020	2021	2022	2023	Total 2014-2018	Total 2014-2023
Unemployment compensation	93	76	53	46	43	42	43	46	50	53	57	59	227	492
Earned income and child tax credits	77	80	83	84	83	83	84	73	74	75	77	78	417	794
Family support[b]	24	25	25	25	25	25	25	25	25	25	25	25	123	248
Child nutrition	19	21	22	22	23	24	25	26	27	28	29	30	117	257
Foster care	7	7	7	7	7	7	7	8	8	8	8	8	36	76
Miscellaneous tax credits[c]	7	6	6	6	6	6	7	0	0	0	0	0	31	31
Subtotal	354	349	330	325	330	325	323	315	322	329	342	344	1,633	3,285
Federal Civilian and Military Retirement														
Civilian[d]	87	89	92	94	98	101	104	108	112	115	119	122	489	1,065
Military	49	54	56	57	63	61	58	64	66	68	75	72	294	638
Other	7	7	7	6	7	7	8	9	9	10	10	10	35	83
Subtotal	143	150	154	158	167	169	170	181	187	193	204	205	818	1,786
Veterans[e]														
Income security	56	65	70	72	81	78	74	82	83	84	92	86	375	801
Other	12	13	13	13	14	14	15	16	17	17	19	19	69	157
Subtotal	68	78	83	85	95	92	88	98	100	101	111	105	444	958
Other Programs														
Agriculture	12	23	15	16	16	16	15	16	16	16	16	16	78	158
Troubled Asset Relief Program	25	-13	3	2	1	1	*	*	*	*	0	0	7	7
Higher education	-19	-18	-22	-20	-12	-3	3	4	4	3	3	3	-54	-36
Deposit insurance	7	7	-9	-10	-11	-12	-13	-18	-18	-13	-14	-15	-54	-131

	Actual,												Total	
													2014-	2014-
	2012	2013	2014	2015	2016	2017	2018	2019	2020	2021	2022	2023	2018	2023
Other	57	47	56	54	56	56	54	54	53	53	60	60	277	558
Subtotal	82	48	43	42	51	58	60	56	55	60	66	65	254	556
Offsetting Receipts														
Medicare[f]	-85	-90	-96	-97	-102	-111	-121	-131	-139	-149	-162	-176	-527	-1,285
Federal share of federal employees' retirement														
Social Security	-16	-16	-16	-17	-18	-18	-19	-20	-21	-21	-22	-23	-88	-195
Military retirement	-22	-21	-21	-21	-22	-23	-24	-25	-26	-27	-28	-29	-111	-243
Civil service retirement and other	-30	-29	-30	-31	-32	-33	-34	-35	-37	-38	-40	-41	-159	-351
Subtotal	-67	-66	-67	-69	-71	-74	-77	-80	-83	-86	-89	-93	-358	-789
Receipts related to natural resources	-13	-15	-14	-14	-15	-14	-15	-19	-17	-18	-18	-18	-73	-164
MERHCF	-11	-9	-9	-9	-10	-10	-11	-12	-12	-13	-14	-14	-49	-114
Other	-33	-25	-23	-29	-32	-34	-30	-31	-31	-32	-27	-27	-148	-295
Subtotal	-209	-205	-209	-219	-230	-243	-255	-273	-282	-298	-310	-328	-1,154	-2,646
Total	2,031	2,116	2,205	2,342	2,535	2,655	2,768	2,924	3,087	3,263	3,501	3,658	12,504	28,938
Memorandum:														
Mandatory Spending Excluding														
Offsetting Receipts	2,240	2,321	2,414	2,560	2,765	2,897	3,022	3,197	3,369	3,561	3,812	3,986	13,659	31,584
Medicare Spending Net of														
Offsetting Receipts	466	502	509	529	578	596	620	680	728	779	862	903	2,833	6,785

Table 1-3. (Continued)

	Actual,												Total	
													2014-	2014-
	2012	2013	2014	2015	2016	2017	2018	2019	2020	2021	2022	2023	2018	2023
Spending for Major Health Care Programs														
Net of Offsetting Receipts[g]	726	778	840	917	1,033	1,095	1,154	1,246	1,325	1,412	1,532	1,615	5,039	12,169

Source: Congressional Budget Office.

Notes: Data on spending for benefit programs in this table generally exclude administrative costs, which are discretionary.

* = between zero and $500 million; MERHCF = Department of Defense Medicare-Eligible Retiree Health Care Fund (including TRICARE for Life).

[a] Excludes offsetting receipts from premium payments and from payments by states from savings on Medicaid's prescription drug costs.

[b] Includes Temporary Assistance for Needy Families and various programs that involve payments to states for child support enforcement and family support, child care entitlements, and research to benefit children.

[c] Includes outlays for the American Opportunity Tax Credit, the first-time homebuyer credit, and other tax credits.

[d] Includes Civil Service, Foreign Service, Coast Guard, and other, smaller retirement programs as well as annuitants' health care benefits.

[e] Income security includes veterans' compensation, pensions, and life insurance programs. Other benefits are primarily education subsidies.

[f] Includes Medicare premiums and amounts paid by states from savings on Medicaid's prescription drug costs.

[g] Includes Medicare (net of receipts from premiums), Medicaid, the Children's Health Insurance Program, and subsidies offered through new health insurance exchanges and related spending.

That total is $62 billion more than the outlays recorded for 2011, when a $58 billion downward revision of previous estimates and $21 billion in new spending caused the Treasury to record negative outlays of $37 billion for the program. This year, CBO anticipates, the net effect of the TARP will be to reduce the budget deficit by $13 billion, largely because the Treasury sold its shares of AIG stock at prices that were significantly higher than previously anticipated (see Table 1-3). That figure would be $38 billion less than the $25 billion net cost recorded for 2012.[8]

Social Security

Social Security outlays grew by $43 billion (or 6 percent) in fiscal year 2012, primarily because beneficiaries received a 3.6 percent cost-of-living adjustment in January 2012 (which applied to three-quarters of the fiscal year; there was no increase the previous year). In addition, the number of people receiving benefits grew by 2.5 percent. That cost-of-living adjustment also boosted benefits in the first quarter of fiscal year 2013; this January's cost-of-living adjustment was smaller (1.7 percent), as is the estimated increase in the number of beneficiaries (2.4 percent). All told, outlays are projected to increase by the same amount—$43 billion—in 2013 as they did in 2012.

Medicare

Net outlays for Medicare (excluding the effects of the shift in the timing of the first scheduled payments to health plans from fiscal year 2012 into fiscal year 2011) grew by 3 percent (or $16 billion) in 2012—a slower rate of growth than any recorded since 2000. Medicare's outlays will increase by 4 percent (or $21 billion) in 2013, CBO estimates. (Those amounts are net of receipts from premiums paid by the program's beneficiaries.)

Unemployment Compensation

The largest decline in spending in 2012 was for unemployment compensation. The number of people receiving first-time payments of regular unemployment benefits, which peaked in 2009 at 14.4 million, continued to fall in 2012, totaling 8.7 million. As a result, outlays for unemployment compensation dropped by $26 billion last year, to $93 billion. The decline is expected to continue—to $76 billion in 2013—as fewer of the long-term unemployed will be in states that qualify to provide the maximum number of weeks of emergency and extended unemployment benefits.[9]

Medicaid

Medicaid spending also declined in 2012—by $24 billion (or 9 percent)—primarily because a temporary increase in the federal share of the program's costs expired in June 2011. That increase initially took effect in 2009 under the American Recovery and Reinvestment Act of 2009 (ARRA, P.L. 111-5) and was extended in modified form through June 2011; it was therefore not in place in fiscal year 2012. In 2013, Medicaid outlays will increase by $15 billion (or 6 percent), CBO estimates.

The Making Work Pay Tax Credit

This refundable tax credit (which expired at the end of December 2010) amounted to 6.2 percent of an eligible individual's earned income for tax years 2009 and 2010 (up to a maximum of $400 for individuals or $800 for joint filers). Because it was refundable, any portion that exceeded an individual's tax liability was paid to that person and recorded as an outlay in the budget. Because the credit expired, its associated outlays fell by $14 billion between fiscal year 2011 and fiscal year 2012.

Other Mandatory Spending

Spending for all other mandatory programs rose by $7 billion from 2011 to 2012 (after adjusting for the shift in certain payments). In 2013, other mandatory spending is anticipated to rise by about $35 billion (or 8 percent), in part because of an increase in spending for agriculture programs ($11 billion).

Discretionary Spending

In fiscal year 2012, total discretionary budget authority (that is, the authority provided in appropriation acts to incur financial obligations that will result in immediate or future outlays) dropped by $23 billion (or 2 percent). Discretionary outlays fell by $62 billion (or 5 percent) in 2012—only the fourth time since 1962 that such outlays have fallen. The decline was divided about equally between defense and nondefense outlays and stemmed mostly from the waning of spending from funds provided in ARRA and from a reduction in spending for military operations and related activities in Afghanistan and Iraq. In 2013, discretionary budget authority is set to drop by another $58 billion (or 5 percent) to $1,140 billion. The automatic spending reductions put in place by the Budget Control Act will reduce funding by $71 billion, and on an annualized basis, funding for war-related activities, primarily in Afghanistan, will fall by $27 billion in 2013, CBO estimates.

Partially offsetting those reductions is $50 billion in funding provided in response to Hurricane Sandy. Funding for all other discretionary programs is $10 billion lower than in the previous year. Total discretionary outlays will fall by $72 billion (or 6 percent) in the current year, CBO projects. The caps on discretionary budget authority in place for 2013 apply to security and nonsecurity categories, rather than to defense and nondefense categories (which apply for the years between 2014 and 2021).[10] Currently, the amount of funding provided in 2013 for each category exceeds the amount allowed by the caps—by $6.8 billion for security and by $1.0 billion for nonsecurity, CBO estimates (see Table 1-4).

CBO's Baseline Budget Projections for 2014 to 2023

CBO constructs its baseline in accordance with provisions set forth in the Balanced Budget and Emergency Deficit Control Act of 1985 and the Congressional Budget and Impoundment Control Act of 1974. For the most part, those laws require that the baseline projections incorporate the assumption that current laws governing taxes and spending in future years are fully implemented. Under those assumptions, CBO projects that the budget deficit will continue to shrink relative to the size of the economy—from 3.7 percent of GDP next year to a low of 2.4 percent by 2015. In dollar terms, the deficit is projected to fall roughly by half between 2013 and 2015. Beginning in 2016, the deficit is projected to increase again both in dollar terms and as a share of the economy, measuring 3.8 percent of GDP by 2023. For the 2014–2023 period, revenues and outlays alike are projected to be above their 40-year averages as a percentage of GDP (see Figure 1-2). Under CBO's baseline projections, most of the decline in the deficit in the next two years is the result of a projected significant rise in revenues, which are estimated to increase by 25 percent between 2013 and 2015. As a share of GDP, revenues in the baseline rise from 16.9 percent in 2013 to 19.1 percent in 2015, resulting about equally from changes in tax rules and from other factors related mainly to the strengthening economy. CBO projects that revenues will remain at about 19 percent of GDP for the rest of the 10-year period. In CBO's baseline, outlays initially decline slightly as a percentage of GDP, from 21.7 percent in 2014 to a low of 21.5 percent in 2017, and then follow an upward trend thereafter, reaching 22.9 percent by the end of the decade. Because of the aging of the population, rising health care costs, and a significant expansion in eligibility for federal subsidies for health insurance, outlays for Social Security and the federal government's major health care programs are projected to rise substantially relative to the size of the economy over the next 10 years. In addition, growing debt and rising interest rates will boost net interest payments. Spending on all other programs—in the aggregate—is projected to decline relative to GDP between 2014 and 2023, primarily because of improving economic conditions and the spending limits in current law.

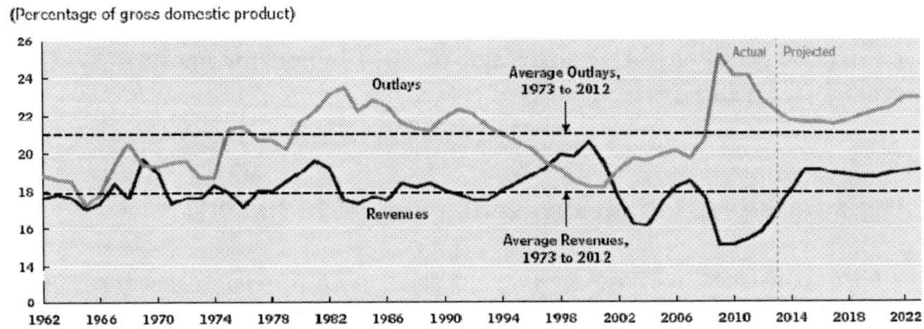

Source: Congressional Budget Office.

Figure 1-2. Total Revenues and Outlays.

Revenues

CBO projects that, if current tax laws remain unchanged, revenues will rise relative to GDP over the next two years and then remain at about 19 percent of GDP through 2023. After 2015, increases in individual income tax receipts relative to GDP will roughly offset projected declines in corporate income tax receipts and declines in remittances from the Federal Reserve as a share of GDP.

Individual Income Taxes

CBO projects that, under current law, individual income tax receipts will rise from $1.3 trillion this year to $2.5 trillion in 2023—or from 7.9 percent to 9.8 percent of GDP. The projected increase in receipts relative to the economy in CBO's baseline reflects real (inflation-adjusted) bracket creep, the economic expansion, recent and scheduled changes in tax provisions, and other factors. In previous baselines, CBO had projected that those receipts would increase to a much higher percentage of GDP by the early part of the next decade, but the American Taxpayer Relief Act's permanent extension of most of the expiring income tax reductions has significantly reduced the amount of revenues anticipated under current law.

Table 1-4. Limits on Discretionary Budget Authority for 2013 (Millions of dollars)

	Security[a]	Nonsecurity[a]	Total
Caps for 2013 in the Deficit Control Act[b]	684,000	359,000	1,043,000
Adjustments			
Overseas contingency operations[c]	99,941	0	99,941
Emergency[d]	7,015	34,627	41,642
Disaster relief[e]	11,779	0	11,779
Program integrityf	0	483	483
Total	118,735	35,110	153,845
Adjusted Caps for 2013	802,735	394,110	1,196,845
Budget Authority as Estimated by			
CBO When the Legislation Was Enacted[g]	809,572	395,133	1,204,705
Amount by Which Budget Authority			
Exceeds the Caps	6,837	1,023	7,860
Memorandum:			
Budget Authority in CBO's Baseline			
Excluding automatic spending reductions and reductions to meet the caps[g,h]	809,026	409,900	1,218,926
Automatic spending reductions[i]	-50,828	-20,522	-71,350
Reductions to meet the caps	-6,837	-1,023	-7,860
Total	751,361	388,355	1,139,716

Source: Congressional Budget Office.

[a] For 2013, the security category comprises discretionary appropriations for the Departments of Defense, Homeland Security, and Veterans Affairs; the National Nuclear Security Administration; the intelligence community management account (Treasury account 95-0401-0-1-054); and discretionary accounts related to international affairs (budget function 150). The nonsecurity category comprises all other discretionary appropriations.

[b] The Budget Control Act of 2011 amended the Balanced Budget and Emergency Deficit Control Act of 1985 to reinstate caps on discretionary budget authority. The American Taxpayer Relief Act of 2012 reduced the caps on security and nonsecurity funding for 2013 by $2 billion each (and reduced the caps on defense and nondefense funding for 2014 by $4 billion each). In addition, automatic procedures are slated to go into effect on March 1 to reduce discretionary funding in 2013 by another $71,350 million, CBO estimates.

[c] This category consists of funding for war-related activities in Afghanistan or for similar activities.

[d] This category consists mostly of funding for relief and recovery from Hurricane Sandy that was designated as an emergency requirement by the Congress. About $5 billion in funding related to Hurricane Sandy was declared disaster relief, and about $3 billion was not declared either as an emergency requirement or as disaster relief. Another $0.5 billion was provided for the Social Services Block Grant program and is classified as mandatory spending in CBO's baseline.

[e] For the purposes of adjustments to the cap, disaster relief refers to activities carried out pursuant to section 102(2) of the Robert T. Stafford Disaster Relief and Emergency Assistance Act; such activities may result from a natural disaster that causes damage of sufficient severity to warrant federal assistance.

[f] Program integrity initiatives identify and reduce overpayments in benefit programs, such as Disability Insurance, Supplemental Security Income, Medicare, Medicaid, and the Children's Health Insurance Program. For 2013, funding for program integrity initiatives thus far has been provided only for Disability Insurance and Supplemental Security Income.

[g] Through March 27, 2013, federal agencies are operating under the Continuing Appropriations Resolution, 2013. The figures in this table are generally annualized totals based on the provisions of that law as modified by the American Taxpayer Relief Act of 2012 and the Disaster Relief Appropriations Act, 2013. The totals exclude the effects of the automatic spending reductions and reductions to meet this year's caps on discretionary budget authority.

[h] The amount of budget authority in CBO's baseline does not match the amount that CBO estimated when the continuing resolution was enacted, for two main reasons. First, nearly $20 billion in savings from changes to mandatory programs included in the resolution was credited against discretionary spending when the legislation was enacted; in CBO's baseline, those savings appear in their normal mandatory accounts. Second, current estimates of receipts of the Federal Housing Administration are about $4 billion higher than the amounts initially credited to the legislation.

[i] As specified in the Budget Control Act, the automatic spending reductions will be allocated between defense and nondefense spending. For this table, CBO has apportioned those amounts to the security and nonsecurity categories.

Real Bracket Creep

Increases in real income will push more income into higher tax brackets, which boosts revenues relative to GDP in CBO's projections by 0.9 percentage points over the next decade.[11]

Economic Recovery

CBO expects that the economic expansion and related factors will cause taxable incomes to rise faster than GDP, boosting individual income tax revenues as a share of GDP by about 0.4 percentage points over the next decade; most of that effect will occur by 2017. Certain components of taxable income— including wages and salaries, capital gains realizations, interest income, and proprietors' income—declined as a share of GDP over the past several years. CBO expects that, as the economy recovers, such income will rebound more quickly than the economy as a whole, increasing revenues as a percentage of GDP. (For more detail, see "Projections of Income" in Section 2.)

Changes in Tax Provisions

Several recent and scheduled changes in tax rules will, on net, increase individual income tax revenues as a share of GDP by 0.2 percentage points, CBO projects. Most significant are tax rates that apply to high-income individuals, which increased in January 2013 both because the American Taxpayer Relief Act did not extend the lower tax rates for those taxpayers and because a new surtax on investment income, enacted in the Affordable Care Act, takes effect in 2013.[12] In addition, for certain higher-income taxpayers, the American Taxpayer Relief Act reinstated limitations on the use of personal exemptions and itemized deductions. CBO expects that those changes will increase revenues as a percentage of GDP in fiscal year 2013 and will raise revenues even more, relative to GDP, in 2014, when they are first in effect for a full fiscal year. That impact persists through the next decade in CBO's baseline projections.

Other Factors

CBO estimates that other factors will increase individual income tax revenues, measured as a share of GDP, by 0.5 percentage points. Those factors include rapid growth in taxable distributions from tax-deferred retirement accounts (such as individual retirement accounts and 401(k) plans) as the population ages. CBO also expects that wages and salaries of higher-income taxpayers will grow faster than those of other taxpayers, boosting average tax rates.

Social Insurance Taxes

CBO expects that, under current law, receipts from social insurance taxes (which are dedicated to funding Medicare, Social Security, other retirement programs, and unemployment benefits) will edge up from 5.9 percent of GDP this year to 6.1 percent in 2014, and then remain at about 6.0 percent of GDP thereafter. The principal source of the initial increase in revenues relative to GDP is the expiration of the payroll tax cut that was in effect in calendar years 2011 and 2012. The employee's share of the tax was reduced by 2 percentage points (from 6.2 percent of wages to 4.2 percent) for those years, reducing receipts in fiscal years 2011 through 2013.

Social insurance receipts will remain stable as a percentage of GDP after 2014, CBO projects, reflecting the offsetting effects of a projected increase in wages and salaries relative to GDP and a projected decrease in social insurance receipts relative to wages and salaries.

CBO expects that wages and salaries, which have declined as a share of GDP since 2009 as they have generally over the past few decades, will grow faster than the economy over the next 10 years, although remaining below their average share of GDP in recent decades. Social insurance receipts, however, are expected to decline relative to wages and salaries because a growing share of earnings is anticipated to be above the taxable maximum amount for Social Security payroll taxes. (That amount, currently $113,700, is indexed to the growth of average wages.) In addition, CBO expects receipts from unemployment insurance taxes, which include state unemployment taxes, to decline to more typical levels in coming years; those taxes have been higher than normal in recent years as states have raised their tax rates and tax bases to replenish unemployment insurance trust funds.

Corporate Income Taxes

Under current law, receipts from corporate income taxes will climb sharply relative to GDP over the next several years, CBO projects—from 1.6 percent this year to 2.5 percent in 2015 and 2.6 percent in 2016 and 2017—before declining to 2.0 percent of GDP by 2023, about the average of the past 40 years.

The average tax rate on domestic economic profits has been low by historical standards for the past several years. Temporary changes to the tax code, including provisions that allowed businesses to accelerate their deductions for equipment purchases, have contributed. CBO projects that the scheduled expiration under current law of those and certain other tax provisions, such as the research and experimentation tax credit, will raise corporate income tax receipts as a share of GDP by about 0.4 percentage points over the next two years. CBO expects that other factors contributing to the low average tax rate on domestic economic profits, such as deductions for bad debts (which have been high by historical standards), will gradually dissipate as the economy recovers, boosting revenues, measured as a share of GDP, by about 0.5 percentage points by 2015.

Between 2017 and 2022, corporate income tax receipts will decline by 0.6 percentage points of GDP, CBO projects, reducing those receipts to 2.0 percent of GDP in 2023. That decline stems largely from an expected drop in domestic economic profits relative to GDP, which in turn results from the rising burden of corporate interest payments, depreciation on the larger stock of business capital, and growth in the share of income going to labor.

Earnings of the Federal Reserve System

Income produced by the various activities of the Federal Reserve System, minus the costs of generating that income and the system's operations, is remitted to the Treasury and counted as revenue. Over the past several years, the Federal Reserve has more than tripled the size of its asset holdings through significant purchases of Treasury securities and mortgage-backed securities issued by Fannie Mae, Freddie Mac, and Ginnie Mae. Those actions caused remittances from the Federal Reserve to climb from 0.2 percent of GDP in 2009 to about 0.5 percent of GDP from 2010 through 2012, where they are expected to remain in 2013.

CBO expects those earnings to edge higher in 2014 and 2015, to about 0.6 percent of GDP, as the Federal Reserve further increases its holdings of Treasury and mortgage-backed securities. Beyond 2015, CBO expects remittances from the Federal Reserve to decline, falling to zero between 2018 and 2020.[13] That drop reflects expected sales of assets by the Federal Reserve as the economy grows to near its potential, which would generate capital losses as interest rates rise. Also expected is an increase in the federal funds rate, which would sharply boost the Federal Reserve's costs of paying interest on reserves of depository institutions.[14] The higher interest rates anticipated after 2015 would initially have a limited effect on earnings from the securities held by the central bank, because it would only gradually purchase new securities earning the higher yields.

In CBO's baseline projections, the Federal Reserve begins remittances to the Treasury again in 2021 that increase thereafter, growing to 0.2 percent of GDP by 2023, about the average in the decade from 2001 through 2010. CBO expects that several factors will contribute to the increase in remittances, including the end of asset sales and their associated losses, a reduction in interest payments on reserves as reserves fall back to more normal levels, and a gradual increase in the share of the portfolio consisting of higher-yielding securities as the portfolio begins to grow again.

Receipts from Other Sources

The federal government also collects revenues from excise taxes, estate and gift taxes, customs duties, and miscellaneous levies. CBO projects that receipts from those sources will rise from 1.0 percent of GDP in 2013 and 2014 to 1.2 percent of GDP in 2015, mainly as a result of new excise taxes and miscellaneous levies enacted in the Affordable Care Act. Revenues from other sources edge downward in CBO's projections to 1.1 percent of GDP after

2017, mostly because improved fuel efficiency of cars and trucks is expected to reduce receipts from excise taxes on motor fuels.

Outlays

The Deficit Control Act requires CBO's projections for most mandatory programs to be made in keeping with the assumption that current laws continue unchanged.[15] Thus, CBO's baseline projections for mandatory programs reflect the automatic enforcement procedures of the Budget Control Act and expected changes in the economy, demographics, and other factors. For discretionary spending, CBO's baseline incorporates the caps put in place by the Budget Control Act and accounts for further reductions in such spending that are scheduled to occur under the act's automatic enforcement procedures. On that basis, total outlays are projected to decline slightly relative to GDP between 2014 and 2017 and then to rise in most years through 2023—averaging 22.1 percent over the decade, slightly above the 21.0 percent of GDP that has been the average for the past 40 years.[16]

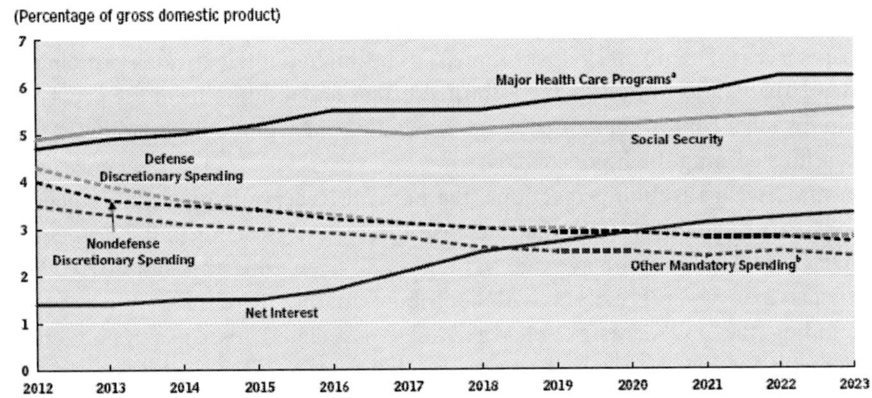

Source: Congressional Budget Office.

[a] Includes Medicare (net of receipts from premiums), Medicaid, the Children's Health Insurance Program, and subsidies offered through new health insurance exchanges and related spending.

[b] Other than mandatory spending for major health care programs and Social Security.

Figure 1-3. Projected Spending in Major Budget Categories.

In CBO's baseline, three major categories of spending are increasing relative to the size of the economy, particularly in the latter part of the 10-year period:

- Under current law, outlays for Social Security will total 5.1 percent of GDP this year and stay near that percentage for the next few years but reach 5.5 percent of GDP by 2023.
- Outlays for the major health care programs— Medicare (net of receipts from premiums), Medicaid, the Children's Health Insurance Program (CHIP), and subsidies offered through new health insurance exchanges and related spending—will soon be even greater than outlays for Social Security. Spending for major health care programs will be nearly 5 percent of GDP in 2013, and such spending is projected to grow rapidly when provisions of the Affordable Care Act are fully implemented by middecade, reaching 6.2 percent of GDP in 2023.
- Net interest is currently equal to 1.4 percent of GDP, but, in CBO's baseline, rising interest rates push that total to 3.3 percent of GDP in 2023.

By the end of the projection period, those three growing categories of spending will be the three largest in the budget (see Figure 1-3). Under current law, over the next 10 years, all other broad categories of spending—for defense and nondefense discretionary programs as well as for other mandatory programs—are projected to decline relative to GDP.

Mandatory Spending

Between 2014 and 2020, mandatory spending (net of offsetting receipts, which reduce outlays) is projected to remain about the same as a share of the economy—between 13.2 percent and 13.5 percent. But, CBO projects, under current law, mandatory spending will accelerate in the final few years of the projection period, reaching 14.1 percent in 2022. Most of the government's mandatory spending consists of outlays for Social Security and the federal government's major health care programs. Those outlays are projected to grow from 10.2 percent in 2014 to 11.7 percent in 2023, accounting for about half of all federal spending by the end of the period.

Social Security and Medicare

Spending for Social Security and Medicare as a percentage of GDP is projected to remain roughly unchanged over the first half of the projection period but to grow more rapidly than the economy in the second half as the rate of growth in GDP declines slightly and as the rate of growth in Medicare spending picks up. Social Security outlays, which are estimated to account for almost one-fourth of the government's spending in 2014, are projected to remain near 5.0 percent of GDP in most years through 2018 and then climb in the following years to reach 5.5 percent of GDP in 2023. Medicare spending (net of receipts from premiums) in CBO's baseline remains around 3.0 percent of GDP through 2019 and then grows to 3.5 percent by 2023.

Medicaid and Other Health Care Programs

Under current law, federal outlays for Medicaid will rise steadily as a share of GDP over the next 10 years, from 1.8 percent in 2014 to 2.2 percent in 2023, by CBO's estimate. That rise is attributable in part to expected increases in the cost of Medicaid's benefits per beneficiary and in part to the fact that many states are expected to expand Medicaid coverage significantly, in keeping with provisions of the Affordable Care Act. In addition, spending on subsidies that will help people purchase health insurance through exchanges (which will become available starting in 2014 for individuals and families who meet income and other eligibility criteria), along with related spending, is projected to increase from 0.1 percent of GDP in 2014 to 0.5 percent 10 years from now.[17]

Other Mandatory Spending

In contrast, as the economy and the labor market gradually improve and as temporary measures that have provided additional assistance expire, spending on all mandatory programs other than Social Security and the major health care programs is projected to fall relative to GDP over the next 10 years, from 3.1 percent in 2014 to 2.4 percent in 2023. Spending for income support programs (such as unemployment compensation, the refundable portion of the earned income and child tax credits, and the Supplemental Nutrition Assistance Program) accounts for nearly all of that decline, gradually falling as a percentage of GDP from 2.0 percent in 2014 to 1.3 percent by 2023, CBO projects. Spending for the remaining mandatory programs is projected to remain near 1 percent of GDP.

Discretionary Spending

In CBO's baseline projections, most appropriations between 2014 and 2021 are assumed to be constrained by the caps and automatic spending reductions put in place by the Budget Control Act. For the final two years—2022 and 2023—discretionary funding covered by the caps is assumed to grow from the 2021 level at the rate of inflation, consistent with the statutory rules governing the baseline. Funding for war-related activities and for some other purposes is not constrained by the caps and is generally assumed to grow with inflation from the amount appropriated for 2013 (see Table 1-4 on page 19 for the amount of such adjustments).[18]

The components of CBO's projections of discretionary spending can be seen in Table 1-5, which shows what discretionary spending would be if appropriations grew at the rate of inflation and how those amounts are affected by the imposition of the caps and by the automatic spending reductions that are scheduled to reduce those caps. As a result of the caps and automatic reductions, projected spending in the baseline for the 2014–2023 period is about $1.5 trillion less than the amount that would be provided if appropriations grew at the rate of inflation after 2013.

Under the assumption that appropriations subject to the caps for 2013 and 2014 will be at the maximum amounts allowed under the Budget Control Act, discretionary budget authority will fall by $17 billion (or 1.5 percent) from 2013 to 2014, CBO estimates. That reduction reflects a full year's implementation of the automatic spending reductions in 2014, compared with the smaller reductions currently in effect for 2013 as a result of the American Taxpayer Relief Act.

After 2014, the resulting caps will limit growth in budget authority for most discretionary programs. Under the assumption that the maximum amounts allowed by the caps are appropriated (and that funding for war-related activities and emergencies grows at the rate of inflation), budget authority in the baseline grows by an average of 2.4 percent annually. Discretionary outlays are projected to grow more slowly—at an average rate of 2.2 percent per year from 2015 through 2023 (which is less than half of the projected growth rate of nominal GDP). Projected outlays during those years grow more slowly than budget authority because they also reflect, with a lag, the reductions in funding in years before 2014. With funding as assumed in the baseline, discretionary outlays would fall to 5.5 percent of GDP by 2023, more than 3 percentage points below their average from 1973 to 2012. Specifically, defense outlays in 2023 would equal 2.8 percent of GDP, compared with a 40-year average of 4.7 percent, and nondefense outlays in 2023 would equal 2.7 percent of GDP, compared with a 40-year average of 4.0 percent.

Net Interest

The increase in debt (in dollar terms), along with an anticipated substantial rise in interest rates as the economy strengthens, is expected to sharply boost interest payments on the debt. CBO projects that, under current law, the government's yearly net interest spending will double as a share of GDP—

from 1.5 percent in 2014 to 3.3 percent in 2023, a percentage that has been exceeded only once in the past 50 years.

Federal Debt Held by the Public

Debt held by the public consists mostly of securities that the Treasury issues to raise cash to fund the federal government's activities and to pay off its maturing liabilities.[19] The amount the Treasury borrows by selling securities (net of the amount of maturing securities that it redeems) is influenced primarily by the annual budget deficit. However, several factors—collectively labeled other means of financing and not directly included in budget totals—also affect the government's need to borrow from the public. Among them are reductions (or increases) in the government's cash balance and in the cash flows associated with federal credit programs (such as those related to student loans and mortgage guarantees) because only the subsidy costs of those programs (calculated on a present-value basis) are reflected in the budget deficit.

CBO projects that Treasury borrowing will be $104 billion more than the projected budget deficit in fiscal year 2013, mainly to finance student loans. Each year from 2014 to 2023, borrowing by the Treasury is expected to exceed the amount of the deficit, mostly because of the need to provide financing for student loans and other credit programs. CBO projects that the government will need to borrow $76 billion more per year, on average, during that period than the budget deficits would suggest. After accounting for all of the government's borrowing needs under current law, CBO projects that debt held by the public will increase from 73 percent of GDP at the end of fiscal year 2012 to 76 percent this year and 78 percent in 2014. Under the assumptions that govern CBO's baseline, debt will fall to a low of 73 percent in 2018 and then rise for the remainder of the projection period, measuring 77 percent of GDP at the end of 2023 (see Table 1-6 on page 28). Along such a path, federal debt held by the public will equal a greater percentage of GDP than in any year between 1951 and 2012 and will be far above the average of 39 percent over the 1973–2012 period. Moreover, it will be on an upward trend by the end of the decade. Debt that is high by historical standards and heading higher will have significant consequences for the budget and the economy:

- The nation's net interest costs will be very high (after interest rates return to more normal levels) and rising. Higher costs for interest eventually will require the government to raise taxes, reduce benefits and services, or undertake some combination of those two actions.

- National saving will be held down, leading to more borrowing from abroad and less domestic investment, which in turn will decrease income in the United States relative to what it would be otherwise.
- Policymakers' ability to use tax and spending policies to respond to unexpected challenges, such as economic downturns, natural disasters, or financial crises will be constrained. As a result, unexpected events could have worse effects on the economy and people's well-being than they would otherwise.
- The likelihood of a fiscal crisis will be higher. During such a crisis, investors would lose so much confidence in the government's ability to manage its budget that the government would be unable to borrow funds at affordable interest rates.

Those consequences would be exacerbated if federal debt exceeded the amounts projected in CBO's baseline, as it would if certain deficit-reducing policies that are scheduled to take effect were instead reversed without being replaced by other policies with similar budgetary effects. Those consequences could be mitigated, however, if policies were enacted that reduced federal debt relative to GDP during the coming decade and beyond.

Other measures of the federal government's financial position are sometimes used. *Debt held by the public excluding financial assets* subtracts from debt the value of the government's financial assets, such as student loans. Under the assumptions for CBO's baseline, that measure will be smaller than debt held by the public alone but will vary roughly in line with it.

Gross federal debt consists of debt held by the public and debt issued to government accounts (for example, the Social Security trust funds). The latter type of debt does not directly affect the economy and has no net impact on the budget.

Under current law, debt held by the public is expected to increase by more than 75 percent between 2012 and 2023, and debt held by government accounts is expected to rise by nearly 30 percent. As a result, gross federal debt is projected to reach $26.1 trillion at the end of 2023.

A similar measure, *debt subject to limit,* is the amount of debt that is subject to the statutory limit on federal borrowing; it includes virtually all gross federal debt. Under the assumptions that govern CBO's baseline, the agency projects that debt subject to limit will reach $26.1 trillion at the end of 2023.

Table 1-5. Discretionary Spending Projected in CBO's Baseline

	2014	2015	2016	2017	2018	2019	2020	2021	2022	2023	Total, 2014-2023
Defense											
Increase discretionary appropriations for 2013											
subject to the caps at the rate of inflation[a]	569	584	600	617	635	653	671	689	n.a.	n.a.	n.a.
Reduction to meet the caps	-17	-18	-23	-27	-32	-37	-41	-45	n.a.	n.a.	n.a.
Caps established by the Budget Control Act	552	566	577	590	603	616	630	644	n.a.	n.a.	n.a.
Automatic spending reductions[b]	-55	-55	-55	-55	-55	-55	-55	-55	n.a.	n.a.	n.a.
Caps with automatic spending reductions[b]	497	511	522	535	548	561	575	589	n.a.	n.a.	n.a.
Adjustments to the caps											
War-related spending	90	92	94	96	99	101	103	105	n.a.	n.a.	n.a.
Emergency designation	*	*	*	*	*	*	*	*	n.a.	n.a.	n.a.
Subtotal, Adjustments	90	92	94	96	99	101	103	106	n.a.	n.a.	n.a.
Total, Defense[c]	588	603	617	632	647	662	679	695	713	731	6,566
Nondefense											
Increase discretionary appropriations for 2013											
subject to the caps at the rate of inflation[a]	522	536	552	568	587	605	622	639	n.a.	n.a.	n.a.
Reduction to meet the caps	-16	-16	-22	-27	-34	-39	-44	-49	n.a.	n.a.	n.a.
Caps established by the Budget Control Act	506	520	530	541	553	566	578	590	n.a.	n.a.	n.a.
Automatic spending reductionsb	-37	-37	-36	-36	-35	-34	-33	-32	n.a.	n.a.	n.a.
Caps with automatic spending reductions[b]	469	483	494	505	518	532	545	558	n.a.	n.a.	n.a.

	2014	2015	2016	2017	2018	2019	2020	2021	2022	2023	Total, 2014-2023
Adjustments to the caps											
War-related spending	11	12	12	12	13	13	13	14	n.a.	n.a.	n.a.
Disaster reliefd	12	12	11	9	9	9	10	10	n.a.	n.a.	n.a.
Emergency designation	42	43	44	44	45	46	47	48	n.a.	n.a.	n.a.
Program integrity	*	1	1	1	1	1	1	1	n.a.	n.a.	n.a.
Subtotal, Adjustments	66	67	67	66	68	69	71	73	n.a.	n.a.	n.a.
Total, Nondefensec	535	550	560	571	586	600	616	631	647	663	5,960
All Defense and Nondefense Budget Authority											
Increase discretionary appropriations for 2013											
subject to the caps at the rate of inflation[a]	1,091	1,120	1,152	1,185	1,222	1,258	1,293	1,328	n.a.	n.a.	n.a.
Reduction to meet the caps	-33	-34	-45	-54	-66	-76	-85	-94	n.a.	n.a.	n.a.
Caps established by the Budget Control Act	1,058	1,086	1,107	1,131	1,156	1,182	1,208	1,234	n.a.	n.a.	n.a.
Automatic spending reductionsb	-92	-91	-91	-91	-90	-89	-88	-87	n.a.	n.a.	n.a.
Caps with automatic spending reductions[b]	966	995	1,016	1,040	1,066	1,093	1,120	1,147	n.a.	n.a.	n.a.
Adjustments to the caps	156	159	161	163	167	170	174	178	n.a.	n.a.	n.a.
Total Discretionary Budget Authority[c]	1,122	1,154	1,177	1,203	1,233	1,263	1,295	1,326	1,359	1,394	12,525
	Outlays										
Defense											
Increase discretionary appropriations for 2013											

Table 1-5. (Continued)

	2014	2015	2016	2017	2018	2019	2020	2021	2022	2023	Total, 2014-2023
subject to the caps at the rate of inflation[a]	577	577	593	604	615	637	655	673	n.a.	n.a.	n.a.
Reduction to meet the caps	-12	-15	-20	-24	-29	-34	-38	-42	n.a.	n.a.	n.a.
Outlays under the caps	565	562	573	579	586	603	617	630	n.a.	n.a.	n.a.
Automatic spending reductions[b]	-47	-52	-53	-54	-54	-54	-54	-54	n.a.	n.a.	n.a.
Outlays under the caps with automatic spending reductions[b]	518	510	520	525	532	549	563	576	n.a.	n.a.	n.a.
Adjustments to the caps											
War-related spending	75	86	92	94	96	98	101	103	n.a.	n.a.	n.a.
Emergency designation	*	*	*	*	*	*	*	*	n.a.	n.a.	n.a.
Subtotal, Adjustments	75	86	92	94	96	99	101	103	n.a.	n.a.	n.a.
Total, Defense[c]	593	597	611	619	628	648	663	679	702	714	6,455
Nondefense											
Increase discretionary appropriations for 2013											
subject to the caps at the rate of inflation[a]	593	606	607	621	637	655	673	691	n.a.	n.a.	n.a.
Reduction to meet the caps	-9	-14	-19	-24	-31	-38	-43	-49	n.a.	n.a.	n.a.
Outlays under the caps	583	592	588	596	606	618	630	642	n.a.	n.a.	n.a.
Automatic spending reductions[b]	-29	-34	-35	-36	-35	-35	-34	-33	n.a.	n.a.	n.a.
Outlays under the caps with automatic spending reductions[b]	555	559	553	561	571	583	596	610	n.a.	n.a.	n.a.
Adjustments to the caps											
War-related spending	6	9	10	11	12	12	12	13	n.a.	n.a.	n.a.
Disaster relief[d]	6	8	9	10	10	10	10	10	n.a.	n.a.	n.a.
Emergency designation	9	17	25	32	37	40	42	44	n.a.	n.a.	n.a.

	2014	2015	2016	2017	2018	2019	2020	2021	2022	2023	Total, 2014-2023
Program integrity	*	1	1	1	1	1	1	1	n.a.	n.a.	n.a.
Subtotal, Adjustments	22	34	45	54	59	62	65	67	n.a.	n.a.	n.a.
Total, Nondefense[c]	577	593	597	614	630	645	661	677	693	710	6,397
All Defense and Nondefense Outlays											
Increase discretionary appropriations for 2013											
subject to the caps at the rate of inflation[a]	1,169	1,184	1,200	1,224	1,253	1,292	1,328	1,364	n.a.	n.a.	n.a.
Reduction to meet the caps	-21	-29	-39	-49	-60	-71	-81	-91	n.a.	n.a.	n.a.
Outlays under the caps	1,148	1,154	1,161	1,176	1,192	1,221	1,246	1,273	n.a.	n.a.	n.a.
Automatic spending reductions[b]	-75	-85	-89	-90	-90	-89	-88	-87	n.a.	n.a.	n.a.
Outlays under the caps with automatic spending reductions[b]	1,073	1,069	1,072	1,086	1,103	1,132	1,159	1,186	n.a.	n.a.	n.a.
Adjustments to the caps	97	120	136	148	155	161	166	170	n.a.	n.a.	n.a.
Total Discretionary Outlays[c]	1,170	1,189	1,209	1,233	1,257	1,293	1,324	1,356	1,396	1,424 12,852	

Source: Congressional Budget Office.

Note: n.a. = not applicable; * = between zero and $500 million.

[a] Funding for overseas contingency operations, emergencies, disaster relief, and certain program integrity initiatives (which identify and reduce overpayments in certain benefit programs) is not constrained by the statutory caps established by the Budget Control Act of 2011. Such caps were specified through 2021; CBO has extrapolated the totals for 2022 and 2023 on the basis of its projected rate of inflation.

[b] Automatic spending reductions are slated to further reduce the caps for 2014 through 2021.

[c] Because the caps on discretionary appropriations do not extend beyond 2021, CBO has extrapolated the totals for 2022 and 2023 on the basis of its projections of inflation.

[d] Under the Balanced Budget and Emergency Deficit Control Act of 1985 (as amended), the limits on discretionary budget authority can be raised to reflect funding for disaster relief. However, the total increase in the cap in any year for that reason can be no more than the average funding for disaster relief over the previous 10 years (excluding the highest and lowest amounts) plus any amount by which the prior year's appropriation was below the maximum allowable cap adjustment for that year. In CBO's baseline, such funding exceeds the average, beginning in 2017; that adjustment is included in the totals shown for disaster relief.

Table 1-6. Federal Debt Projected in CBO's Baseline (Billions of dollars)

	Actual, 2012	2013	2014	2015	2016	2017	2018	2019	2020	2021	2022	2023
Debt Held by the Public at the Beginning of the Year	10,128	11,280	12,229	12,937	13,462	14,025	14,642	15,316	16,092	16,957	17,876	18,902
Changes in Debt Held by the Public												
Deficit	1,089	845	616	430	476	535	605	710	798	854	957	978
Other means of financing	62	104	93	95	87	82	69	66	66	65	69	64
Total	1,152	949	708	525	563	617	674	776	865	919	1,026	1,041
Debt Held by the Public at the End of the Year	11,280	12,229	12,937	13,462	14,025	14,642	15,316	16,092	16,957	17,876	18,902	19,944
Memorandum:												
Debt Held by the Public at the End of the Year (As a percentage of GDP)	72.5	76.3	77.7	76.3	74.6	73.4	73.1	73.5	74.2	75.0	76.0	77.0
Debt Held by the Public Excluding												
Financial Assets[a]												
In billions of dollars	10,392	11,243	11,833	12,241	12,695	13,211	13,794	14,482	15,259	16,091	17,024	17,977
As a percentage of GDP	66.8	70.1	71.1	69.4	67.6	66.2	65.9	66.2	66.8	67.5	68.5	69.4
Gross Federal Debt[b]	16,048	17,068	17,886	18,501	19,166	19,938	20,793	21,736	22,754	23,810	24,937	26,079
Debt Subject to Limit[c]	16,027	17,047	17,864	18,479	19,143	19,915	20,769	21,711	22,729	23,784	24,911	26,052

Source: Congressional Budget Office. Note: GDP = gross domestic product.

[a] Subtracts from debt held by the public the value of outstanding student loans and other credit transactions, financial assets (such as preferred stock) purchased from institutions participating in the Troubled Asset Relief Program, cash balances, and other financial instruments.

[b] Comprises federal debt held by the public plus Treasury securities held by federal trust funds and other government accounts.

[c] The amount of federal debt that is subject to the overall limit set in law. Debt subject to limit differs from gross federal debt because most debt issued by agencies other than the Treasury and the Federal Financing Bank is excluded from the debt limit. The debt limit was most recently set at $16.4 trillion but has recently been suspended through May 18, 2013.

Changes in CBO's Baseline Since August 2012

Since August 2012, when the agency completed its previous set of baseline projections, CBO has added $204 billion to its estimate of the deficit in 2013 and a total of $4.6 trillion to its baseline projection of the cumulative deficit from 2013 through 2022 (see Appendix A). Legislation enacted in the interim led CBO to boost projected deficits by $4.7 trillion through 2022 (including debt service); almost all of that increase stems from the enactment of the American Taxpayer Relief Act early in January. Also included in that amount is additional emergency spending. As mandated by law, the baseline incorporates the assumption that amounts equal to the $41 billion in emergency funding provided in the wake of Hurricane Sandy are appropriated each year with adjustments for inflation; that assumption added about $340 billion to outlays in the baseline. Revised economic projections increased the projection of the cumulative deficit by $141 billion, whereas other, technical changes reduced the projection of the cumulative deficit by $270 billion.

Uncertainty in Budget Projections

Even if federal laws remained unchanged for the next decade, actual budgetary outcomes would differ from CBO's baseline projections because of unanticipated changes in economic conditions and in a host of other factors that affect federal spending and revenues.

CBO's budgetary projections depend on the agency's economic projections for the coming decade, including forecasts for such variables as interest rates, inflation, and the growth of real GDP. Discrepancies between those forecasts and actual economic outcomes can result in significant differences between baseline budget projections and budgetary outcomes. For instance, CBO's baseline economic forecast anticipates that the interest rate on 3-month Treasury bills—which has hovered near zero for the past several years—will climb to 4 percent by the end of 2017; by that point, the rate on 10-year Treasury notes is also projected to rise from its current level of around 2 percent. If interest rates on all types of Treasury securities were 1 percentage point higher or lower each year from 2014 through 2023 and all other economic variables were unchanged, cumulative outlays projected for the 10-year period would be about $1.1 trillion higher or lower (excluding the additional costs of servicing the federal debt).

Uncertainty also surrounds myriad technical factors that can substantially affect CBO's baseline projections. For example, spending per enrollee for

Medicare and Medicaid—which generally has grown faster than GDP—is very difficult to predict. If per capita costs in those programs rose 1 percentage point faster or slower per year than CBO has projected for the next decade, total outlays for Medicare (net of receipts from premiums) and Medicaid would be about $650 billion higher or lower for that period.

The impact of the Affordable Care Act is another source of great uncertainty. To estimate the effects of the act's broad changes to the nation's health care and health insurance systems, CBO and the staff of the Joint Committee on Taxation (JCT) have made projections concerning an array of technical, behavioral, and economic factors, some of which involve programs and institutions (such as the health insurance exchanges) that do not yet exist.

Projections of revenues also are quite sensitive to uncertainty about economic and technical factors. Revenues depend on total amounts of wages and salaries, corporate profits, and other income, all part of CBO's economic projections. For example, if the growth of real GDP and taxable incomes were 0.1 percentage point lower per year than in CBO's baseline projections, revenues would be lower than in the baseline projections by roughly $275 billion over the 2014–2023 period. In addition, forecasting the amount of revenues that the government will collect from taxpayers for a given quantity of incomes included in the economic projections requires technical assumptions about the distribution of income and about many aspects of taxpayers' behavior. (Taxpayers' behavior, for example, determines the amount of deductions and credits people receive and how much income in the form of capital gains they realize from selling assets.) If CBO's judgments about such behavior and actual outcomes differ, the effect on revenues can be significant. Even relatively small deviations can have a substantial impact on budget deficits. For example, if revenues projected for 2023 were too high by 5 percent (that is, if average annual growth during the coming decade was about 0.5 percentage points less than CBO estimates) and projected outlays for mandatory programs were too low by 5 percent, the deficit for that year would be about $430 billion greater than the $978 billion in CBO's baseline—or 5.4 percent of GDP, rather than 3.8 percent. Outcomes could differ in the other direction as well.

Alternative Assumptions About Fiscal Policy

CBO's baseline budget projections—which are constructed in accordance with provisions of law—are intended to show what would happen to federal spending, revenues, and deficits if current laws generally remained unchanged. Clearly, future legislation could lead to markedly different budget outcomes. Moreover, although the American Taxpayer Relief Act has reduced the number of changes to tax policies that are scheduled to take effect under current law, some significant changes to tax and spending policies alike are still set to occur. As a result, baseline projections constructed on the assumption that current laws will remain in place could differ markedly from the budgetary outcomes that would result if those laws were modified so that current policies were maintained instead.

To assist policymakers and analysts who may hold differing views about the most useful benchmark against which to consider possible changes to laws or policies, CBO has estimated the effects on budget projections of some alternative assumptions about future policies (see Table 1-7). The discussion below focuses on how those policy actions would directly affect revenues and outlays. Such changes also would influence projections of the costs of servicing the federal debt (shown separately in the table).

Military and Diplomatic Operations in Afghanistan and Other War-Related Activities

CBO's projections of discretionary spending for the next 10 years include outlays for military and diplomatic operations in Afghanistan and for other overseas contingency operations. The projections are based on budget authority provided for those purposes in 2012 and in prior years, the $100 billion in budget authority provided for 2013 (the annualized amount provided in the current continuing resolution), and the $1.1 trillion that is projected to be appropriated over the 2014–2022 period (under the assumption that this year's funding will be adjusted for anticipated inflation).

In coming years, the funding required for overseas contingency operations—in Afghanistan or other countries—may eventually be smaller than the amounts in the baseline if the number of deployed troops and the pace of operations diminish over time. Thus, CBO has formulated a budget scenario that assumes a reduction in the deployment of U.S. forces abroad for military actions and a concomitant reduction in diplomatic operations and foreign aid. Many other scenarios—some costing more and some less—also are possible.

In 2012, the number of U.S. active-duty, Reserve, and National Guard personnel deployed for war-related activities averaged about 115,000, according to CBO's estimates. Under the scenario presented here, the average number of military personnel deployed for war-related purposes would decline over three years: to 85,000 in 2013, 60,000 in 2014, and 45,000 in 2015 and thereafter. (Those numbers could represent various allocations of forces in different places around the world.) Under that scenario, and assuming that the related funding for diplomatic operations and foreign aid declines at a similar rate, discretionary outlays over the 2014–2023 period would be $582 billion less than the $1.1 trillion for overseas contingency operations included in the baseline.

Emergency Funding for Disaster Relief

Recently, lawmakers provided $50 billion in disaster relief in response to Hurricane Sandy. The portion of such funding declared an emergency requirement ($41 billion) is not constrained by the caps and, following the rules governing baseline projections, is assumed to be provided each year, with adjustments for inflation, in CBO's baseline.[20] If, however, such funding was not provided in future years, discretionary outlays would be $302 billion lower between 2014 and 2023 than in the baseline.

Other Discretionary Spending

Policymakers could vary discretionary funding in many ways from the amounts projected in the baseline. For example, if none of the constraints on discretionary funding were implemented and if appropriations grew each year through 2023 at the same rate as inflation after 2013, discretionary spending would be about $1.5 trillion higher for that period than it is in the baseline. If, by contrast, lawmakers kept appropriations constrained by the caps in 2013 at the same nominal level through 2023 (after accounting for the $71 billion reduction that will result from the automatic enforcement procedures set in the Budget Control Act), total discretionary outlays would be $829 billion lower for the period from 2014 through 2023. Under that scenario (sometimes called a freeze in regular appropriations), total discretionary spending would fall from 7.6 percent of GDP in fiscal year 2013 to 4.7 percent in 2023; by comparison, the lowest share for discretionary spending in any year since 1962 (the earliest year for which such data have been reported) was 6.2 percent in 1999.

Medicare's Payments to Physicians

Under current law, spending for Medicare is constrained by a rate-setting system—called the sustainable growth rate—that has existed for several years to control the fees physicians receive for their services. If the system is allowed to operate as currently structured, physicians' fees will be reduced by about 25 percent in January 2014 and will increase by small amounts in subsequent years, CBO projects. If, instead, lawmakers override those scheduled reductions—as they have every year since 2003—spending on Medicare might be greater than the amounts projected in CBO's baseline. For example, holding payment rates through 2023 at the levels they are now would raise outlays for Medicare (net of premiums paid by beneficiaries) by $14 billion in 2014 and about $138 billion (or about 2 percent) between 2014 and 2023.[21] The effect on Medicare (and on the deficit) of making such a change would depend on whether lawmakers offset the effects of the change, as they often have done in the past, with other changes to reduce deficits.

Automatic Enforcement Procedures

The Budget Control Act put in place automatic procedures to reduce discretionary and mandatory spending that are now scheduled to take effect in March 2013 and continue through 2021. If fully implemented, those procedures will require equal reductions (in dollar terms) in defense and nondefense spending.

For 2013, the reductions are to be achieved by automatically canceling, or sequestering, a portion of the budgetary resources for most discretionary programs as well as for some programs and activities that generate mandatory spending.[22]

For the period from 2014 through 2021, the automatic procedures lower the caps on discretionary budget authority specified in the Budget Control Act and impose sequestration for some mandatory spending. If lawmakers chose to prevent those automatic cuts each year without making other changes that reduced spending by offsetting amounts, spending would be $42 billion higher in 2013 and $995 billion (or about 2 percent) higher over the 2014–2023 period than is projected in CBO's current baseline. Total discretionary outlays would be $869 billion (or 6.8 percent) higher, and mandatory outlays would be $126 billion (or 0.4 percent) higher.[23]

Revenues

Although the American Taxpayer Relief Act permanently extended several tax provisions that substantially affected revenues, a host of other tax provisions—many of which have been extended repeatedly—are still scheduled to expire over the next decade (see Box 1-1 on page 12). If all of those provisions were permanently extended, CBO and JCT estimate, revenues would be lower—and, although a much smaller effect, outlays for refundable tax credits would be higher—by a total of about $1.0 trillion over the 2014–2023 period.

Table 1-7. Budgetary Effects of Selected Policy Alternatives Not Included in CBO's Baseline (Billions of dollars)

												Total	
	2013	2014	2015	2016	2017	2018	2019	2020	2021	2022	2023	2014-2018	2014-2023
	Policy Alternatives That Affect Discretionary Outlays												
Reduce the Number of Troops Deployed for Overseas													
Contingency Operations to 45,000 by 2015[a] Effect on the deficit[b]	0	16	37	51	60	64	67	69	71	73	74	228	582
Debt service	0	*	*	2	4	8	11	15	19	23	28	14	111
Remove Extrapolation of Emergency Funding for Disaster Relief[c]													
Effect on the deficit[b]	0	2	9	18	26	33	38	41	43	45	47	88	302
Debt service	0	*	*	*	1	3	5	7	9	11	14	5	51
Increase Regular Discretionary Appropriations at the Rate of Inflation[d]													
Effect on the deficit[b]	-38	-97	-115	-128	-139	-150	-160	-169	-178	-186	-193	-628	-1,514
Debt service	*	-1	-2	-6	-13	-24	-31	-41	-51	-63	-74	-45	-306
Freeze Regular Discretionary Appropriations at the 2013 Amount[e]													
Effect on the deficit[b]	0	-12	*	19	41	63	88	115	141	171	203	110	829
Debt service	0	*	*	*	1	4	7	12	18	26	35	5	103

												Total	
	2013	2014	2015	2016	2017	2018	2019	2020	2021	2022	2023	2014-2018	2014-2023
		Policy Alternative That Affects Mandatory Outlays											
Maintain Medicare's Payment Rates for Physicians at the Current Rate[f]													
Effect on the deficit[b]	0	-14	-16	-13	-12	-12	-13	-14	-14	-15	-16	-67	-138
Debt service	0	*	*	-1	-1	-2	-3	-4	-5	-6	-7	-5	-29
	Policy Alternative That Affects Both Discretionary and Mandatory Outlays												
Remove the Effect of the Automatic Enforcement													
Procedures Specified in the Budget Control Act[g]													
Effect on the deficit[b]	-42	-89	-99	-103	-104	-105	-104	-104	-104	-94	-89	-500	-995
Debt service *	*	-1	-1	-5	-11	-19	-25	-31	-38	-45	-51	-38	-228
	Policy Alternative That Affects the Tax Code[h]												
Extend Expiring Tax Provisions[i]													
Effect on the deficit [b]	*	-58	-98	-89	-83	-81	-102	-103	-108	-114	-120	-408	-954
Debt service	*	*	-1	-4	-8	-15	-19	-25	-32	-38	-46	-28	-188
		Policy Alternative That Affects Spending and Revenues											
Changes in Deficits from the Alternative Fiscal Scenario[j]													
Effect on the deficit[b]	-42	-160	-212	-205	-199	-198	-219	-221	-226	-222	-225	-975	-2,088
Debt service	*	-2	-2	-10	-21	-36	-47	-60	-74	-89	-104	-71	-446
Memorandum:													

Table 1-7. (Continued)

												Total	
	2013	2014	2015	2016	2017	2018	2019	2020	2021	2022	2023	2014-2018	2014-2023
Outlays for Overseas Contingency Operations in CBO's Baseline	129	112	106	106	106	108	110	113	116	119	121	539	1,118
Deficit in CBO's Baseline	-845	-616	-430	-476	-535	-605	-710	-798	-854	-957	-978	-2,661	-6,958
Deficit Under the Alternative Fiscal Scenario	-887	-778	-644	-691	-755	-839	-976	-1,080	-1,154	-1,268	-1,307	-3,707	-9,492

Sources: Congressional Budget Office; staff of the Joint Committee on Taxation.

Notes: Negative numbers indicate an increase in the deficit; positive numbers indicate a decrease in the deficit.

* = between -$500 million and $500 million.

[a] For this alternative, CBO does not extrapolate the $100 billion in budget authority for military operations, diplomatic activities, and foreign aid in Afghanistan and other countries provided for 2013. Rather, the alternative incorporates the assumption that, as the number of troops falls to about 45,000 by 2015, funding for overseas contingency operations declines as well, to $70 billion in 2014, $51 billion in 2015, and then to an average of about $45 billion per year from 2016 on—for a total of $482 billion over the 2014–2023 period. [Note corrected on February 5, 2013, after initial release]

[b] Excludes debt service.

[c] For this alternative, CBO does not extrapolate the $41 billion in budget authority provided for relief and recovery from Hurricane Sandy that was designated as an emergency requirement in the Disaster Relief Appropriations Act, 2013. That act also provided $5 billion in funding designated as disaster funding (as defined in the Budget Control Act of 2011) and $3 billion that was not designated as emergency funding; both types of funding are extrapolated in CBO's baseline, subject to constraints set in the Budget Control Act.

[d] These estimates reflect the assumption that appropriations will not be constrained by caps and other provisions of the Budget Control Act and will instead grow at the rate of inflation from their 2013 level. Discretionary funding related to federal personnel is inflated using the employment cost index for wages and salaries; other discretionary funding is adjusted using the gross domestic product price index.

[e] This alternative reflects the assumption that appropriations for 2013 that are constrained by the caps, minus an estimated reduction of $71 billion resulting from the automatic enforcement procedures for this year, will total $978 billion. Such appropriations would generally be frozen at the 2013 level through 2023.

[f] Medicare's current payment rates for physicians' services are scheduled to drop by 25 percent on January 1, 2014, and will increase by small amounts in subsequent years. In this alternative, payment rates are assumed to continue at their current level through 2023.

[g] The Budget Control Act specified that if lawmakers did not enact legislation originating from the Joint Select Committee on Deficit Reduction that would reduce projected deficits by at least $1.2 trillion, automatic procedures would go into effect to reduce both discretionary and mandatory spending during the 2013–2021 period. Such automatic reductions in spending would take the form of equal cuts (in dollar terms) in funding for defense and nondefense programs in 2013 through 2021. The American Taxpayer Relief Act of 2012 subsequently reduced the amount of savings required in 2013 by $24 billion. For 2013, those reductions would be achieved by automatically canceling a portion of the budgetary resources (in an action known as sequestration) for most discretionary programs and for some programs and activities that generate mandatory spending. For the 2014–2021 period, the automatic procedures lower the caps on discretionary budget authority specified in the Budget Control Act and impose sequestration for some mandatory spending. The budgetary effects of this option cannot be combined with those of any of the alternatives that affect discretionary spending other than the one to reduce the number of troops deployed for overseas contingency operations.

[h] The estimates are mainly from the staff of the Joint Committee on Taxation and are preliminary.

[i] These estimates reflect the impact of extending about 75 provisions. Nearly all of those provisions have been extended previously; some, such as the research and experimentation tax credit, multiple times.

[j] In *The Budget and Economic Outlook: Fiscal Years 2012 to 2022* (January 2012), www.cbo.gov/publication/42905, and the update to that report in August 2012, CBO presented an alternative fiscal scenario that incorporated the assumptions that all expiring tax provisions (other than the payroll tax reduction in effect in calendar years 2011 and 2012) were extended; the alternative minimum tax was indexed for inflation after 2011; Medicare's payment rates for physicians' services were held constant at the 2012 level; and the automatic spending reductions required by the Budget Control Act, which were set to take effect in January 2013, would not occur. The American Taxpayer Relief Act permanently extended many provisions slated to expire at the end of December 2012 and indexed the alternative minimum tax for inflation; therefore, the remaining components of the alternative fiscal scenario consist of holding constant the Medicare payment rates (which are now scheduled to fall in January 2014), undoing the automatic spending reductions (which were reduced by $24 billion and postponed until March 1, 2013), and extending certain tax provisions.

Most of those tax provisions are scheduled to expire at the end of 2013. They include a provision allowing businesses to immediately deduct 50 percent of new investments in equipment, which JCT estimates accounts for about $0.3 trillion of the budgetary effects of extending all the provisions. The budgetary cost of extending all of the tax provisions increases starting in 2019, because the American Taxpayer Relief Act extended through 2017 certain provisions affecting refundable tax credits.

Extending those provisions would increase outlays for refundable credits and reduce revenues by a total of about $140 billion over the 2018–2023 period, mostly starting in 2019 because payments for refundable credits are typically made a year after the applicable tax year.

An Alternative Fiscal Scenario

In recent years, CBO has presented an alternative fiscal scenario that illustrated the impact on projected deficits and debt of maintaining policies that were then in place but that were scheduled to change under then-current law.

That scenario, as described by CBO in *The Budget and Economic Outlook: Fiscal Years 2012 to 2022* and in *An Update to the Budget and Economic Outlook: Fiscal Years 2012 to 2022*, incorporated the assumptions that all expiring tax provisions (other than the payroll tax reduction in effect in calendar years 2011 and 2012) were extended; the AMT was indexed for inflation after 2011; Medicare's payment rates for physicians' services were held constant at the 2012 level; and the automatic spending reductions required by the Budget Control Act, which were set to take effect in January 2013, would not occur.

The American Taxpayer Relief Act extended many of the provisions slated to expire at the end of December 2012 and indexed the AMT for inflation. As a result, many components of the alternative fiscal scenario (including many with the largest budgetary effects) have now been made permanent.

One prominent component— the extension of the lower tax rates on the income of higher-income people originally enacted in 2001 and 2003—was not included in the legislation. The remaining components consist of holding constant Medicare's payment rates (now scheduled to be reduced in January 2014), undoing the automatic spending reductions (which were reduced by $24 billion and postponed until March 1, 2013), and extending certain expiring tax provisions.

If lawmakers were to make those changes to current law, and if other changes in policies with offsetting effects on budget deficits were not enacted, deficits and debt would be significantly higher than the amounts shown in CBO's current baseline.

Relative to the baseline projections for 2014 to 2023, deficits would rise by a total of $2.5 trillion (including debt-service costs) to yield cumulative deficits of $9.5 trillion. Debt held by the public would reach 87 percent of GDP by the end of 2023, the largest share since 1947. Under that scenario, revenues from 2014 to 2023 would average 18.5 percent of GDP (slightly above their 40-year average of 17.9 percent), and outlays would average 22.9 percent (well above their 40-year average of 21.0 percent).

SECTION 2. THE ECONOMIC OUTLOOK

The Congressional Budget Office (CBO) expects that, under current laws governing taxes and spending, economic activity will expand slowly in 2013 but will increase more rapidly in 2014. As measured by the change from the fourth quarter of the previous year, real (inflation-adjusted) gross domestic product (GDP) is projected to increase by 1.4 percent this year and by 3.4 percent next year. With economic growth subdued until 2014, CBO forecasts that the unemployment rate will remain high—above 71/2 percent through next year. If that occurs, 2014 will be the sixth consecutive year with unemployment exceeding 71/2 percent of the labor force, the longest period of such high unemployment in the past 70 years. CBO projects that the high number of unemployed workers and the large amount of other unused resources in the economy will help to keep the rate of inflation (as measured by the price index for personal consumption expenditures, or PCE) below 2 percent during this year and next and that interest rates will stay quite low as well.

That pattern of slow growth in 2013 and then quickening growth in 2014 reflects a combination of a gradual improvement in underlying economic factors and the tightening of federal fiscal policy that is scheduled to occur this year. The effects of the housing and financial crisis will continue to fade, CBO expects: An upswing in housing construction (albeit from a very low level), rising real estate and stock prices, and increasing availability of credit will help to spur a virtuous cycle of faster growth in employment, income, consumer spending, and business investment over the next few years.

However, the federal fiscal policy specified by current law will represent a drag on economic activity this year.

CBO estimates that economic growth in 2013 would be roughly 11/2 percentage points faster than the agency now projects if not for the fiscal tightening. About 11/4 percentage points of that effect come from the automatic reductions in federal spending described in Section 1, the expiration of the cut in payroll tax rates, and the increase in tax rates on income above certain thresholds; the spending changes and the combined tax changes account for about equal portions. The remaining 1/4 percentage point comes from other, smaller changes in spending and taxes. If policymakers modified the tax and spending policies in current law, their actions could have significant implications for economic growth. For instance, less fiscal tightening this year would lead to stronger growth in 2013 but, if not accompanied by sufficient additional tightening in later years, would also restrain real output and income in the middle of the decade and beyond owing to higher federal debt.[1]

Although CBO anticipates faster economic growth after this year, output is likely to remain below its potential (or maximum sustainable) level until 2017—almost a decade after the recession started in December 2007. CBO estimates that real GDP in the fourth quarter of 2012 was below its potential level by about 51/2 percent; that gap is only modestly smaller than the gap (of about 71/2 percent) that existed at the end of the recession in mid-2009 because growth in output since then has been only slightly faster, on average, than growth in potential output (see Figure 2-1). With such a large gap between actual and potential output persisting for so long, the cumulative loss of output relative to the economy's potential between 2007 and 2017 will be equivalent to nearly half of the output produced last year. Consistent with the forecast that output will be growing rapidly enough between 2014 and 2017 to close the output gap, the unemployment rate is projected to fall from about 71/2 percent at the end of 2014 to about 51/2 percent at the end of 2017. The interest rate on three-month. Treasury bills is forecast to remain low through 2015 and then rise considerably through 2017 as the economy strengthens; the interest rate on 10-year Treasury notes is projected to rise steadily through 2017. Beyond 2017, CBO's economic forecast is based on the assumption that real GDP will grow at the same rate as potential GDP, because the agency does not attempt to predict the timing or magnitude of fluctuations in the business cycle so far into the future. Under that assumption, the average growth of real GDP in CBO's projection is 21/4 percent a year during the 2019–2023 period; that pace is much slower than the average annual growth of

31/4 percent since 1950, primarily because of slower expected growth in the labor force from both the retirement of the baby-boom generation and an end to the long-standing increase in the labor force participation of women.

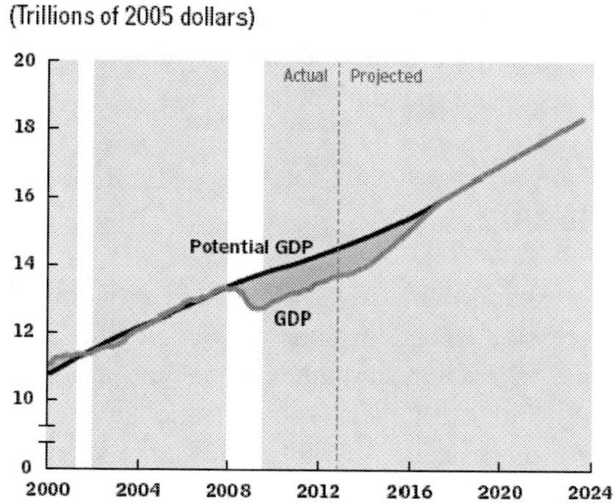

Sources: Congressional Budget Office; Department of Commerce, Bureau of Economic Analysis.

Notes: Potential gross domestic product (GDP) is CBO's estimate of the maximum sustainable level of output of the economy.

Data are quarterly. Actual data are plotted through the third quarter of 2012. Projections are plotted through the fourth quarter of 2023.

Figure 2-1. GDP and Potential GDP.

In addition, the unemployment rate in CBO's projection falls to 5.2 percent by the end of 2023, and inflation holds steady at 2 percent between 2019 and 2023. The interest rate on three-month Treasury bills stabilizes at 4.0 percent in the 2019–2023 period, and the rate on 10-year Treasury notes stabilizes at 5.2 percent. Since the end of the recession, the path of recovery has been difficult to predict, and outcomes in future years will no doubt hold surprises as well. Many developments apart from changes in the laws regarding federal taxes and spending—such as unanticipated changes in the pace of economic growth abroad—could cause economic outcomes to differ substantially from those CBO has projected. CBO's current forecast of economic growth for 2013 differs significantly from the agency's August 2012 forecast. The American Taxpayer Relief Act of 2012 (Public Law 112-240) removed a significant amount of the fiscal tightening that had been scheduled to take effect in January 2013. (For a more detailed examination of that legislation, see Box 1-1 in Section 1.) As a result, CBO no longer projects that real GDP will decline this year.[2] However, CBO's current projection for the growth of real GDP in 2013 is still considerably below those of the *Blue Chip* consensus (which is based on roughly 50 private-sector forecasts) and the Federal Reserve's Federal Open Market Committee. Those differences probably stem in large part from differing assumptions about the federal government's future tax and spending policies.

The Economy in 2012

The economy expanded modestly in 2012, continuing the slow growth seen since the recession ended in June 2009, and the unemployment rate continued to decline.[3] Spending strengthened in some sectors—especially residential investment—but consumers spent cautiously and the advance of business investment moderated. Growth in consumer spending was probably held back by tepid growth in households' income, and growth in business investment was in turn limited by modest gains in consumer spending. In addition, spending was probably restrained by the anticipation of higher taxes and other consequences of fiscal tightening, as well as by uncertainty about the magnitude and composition of that tightening. Despite those negative effects of fiscal policy, the demand for goods and services appeared to gain some momentum in 2012, which will support economic growth going forward. The labor market improved modestly in 2012, although it remains weak—primarily because overall demand for goods and services, and thus businesses' need to hire additional workers, has been growing slowly. In addition, inflation in consumer prices eased, and both short- and long-term interest rates stayed very low.

Economic Growth

On the basis of information available when CBO completed its economic projections in mid-January, the agency estimated that real GDP increased by 1.9 percent in 2012, as measured by the change from the fourth quarter of the previous year, compared with 2.0 percent in 2011. It turned out to be less.[4] Spending by consumers and businesses remained guarded, while residential investment continued to strengthen. In addition, purchases by federal, state, and local governments saw smaller declines than in 2011, and net exports increased slightly.

Consumer Spending

Real spending on consumer goods and services—which represents about two-thirds of all spending in the economy—grew by an estimated 1.9 percent last year, about the same increase as in 2011. Consumer spending has recently been bolstered by gains in households' net worth, reflecting rising house prices, improvement in the stock market, and declines in mortgage debt. However, continued high unemployment has held down the growth of wages and salaries as well as consumers' confidence about future gains in income. Those factors, along with tight credit conditions for many households, have continued to restrain the growth of consumer spending. In addition, spending was probably held down last year by the anticipation of higher taxes and other effects of impending fiscal tightening, as well as by uncertainty about that tightening.

Business Investment

Real business fixed investment— in nonresidential structures, equipment, and software— grew much more slowly last year than in the preceding years: by an estimated 3.3 percent in 2012, following gains of 10.2 percent in 2011 and 7.7 percent in 2010. The slowdown in 2012 probably reflected businesses' response to the weak growth in demand for goods and services; it may also have reflected uncertainty and concern about the significant fiscal tightening that had been scheduled for early 2013. The growth of real investment in equipment and software slowed somewhat more than did the growth of real investment in nonresidential structures. That difference may reflect the fact that businesses can adjust their purchases of equipment and software more rapidly than their spending on structures.

Residential Investment

In 2012, residential investment grew rapidly as recovery in the housing market gained traction. Real residential investment rose by 15.4 percent last year, in CBO's estimation, up steeply from 3.9 percent in 2011—the first annual increase since 2005 (see Figure 2-2). Housing investment is still very low by historical standards, however, and the contribution of such investment to GDP growth remains small because the housing sector accounts for only a minor fraction of output. The recent expansion of housing construction is partly a response to the continued decline in the number of vacant housing units, following sharp increases in that number before and during the recession. Owing to the very low level of construction in recent years, the number of vacant housing units in excess of what would be expected under normal economic conditions fell to 1.2 million, or 0.9 percent of the total stock, in the third quarter of 2012, down from a peak of 2.9 million in the fourth quarter of 2008. Also bolstering housing construction was an improved outlook for house prices, which, in CBO's estimates, climbed by 5.3 percent from the fourth quarter of 2011 to the fourth quarter of 2012.

Governments' Purchases

Purchases by federal, state, and local governments (as measured by the Department of Commerce's national income and product accounts and adjusted to remove the effects of inflation) fell slightly in 2012 but by much less than in 2011. Purchases by the federal government edged down by 0.7 percent last year (as measured on a fourth-quarter-to-fourth-quarter basis), according to CBO's estimates, after falling by 4.2 percent in 2011. For state and local governments, purchases fell by 0.9 percent in 2012, compared with decreases of 2.7 percent in 2011 and 3.6 percent in 2010. The smaller decline in 2012 primarily reflects improvements in state and local governments' finances from stronger growth in tax revenues.

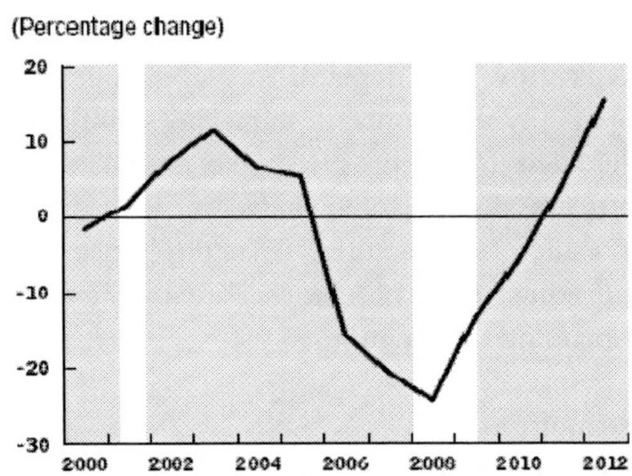

Sources: Congressional Budget Office; Department of Commerce, Bureau of Economic Analysis.

Notes: Real residential investment consists of spending on residential construction, improvements to existing housing, mobile homes, and real estate brokers' commissions, adjusted to remove the effects of inflation.

Data are annual and are plotted through 2012. The value for 2012 reflects CBO's estimate for the fourth quarter. Percentage changes are measured between the fourth quarters of successive years.

Figure 2-2. Real Residential Investment.

Net Exports

International trade added a small amount to the growth of real GDP in 2012, in CBO's estimation. Although the growth rate of real exports decreased, partly in response to ongoing economic problems in the euro zone, that decrease was more than offset by a larger drop in the growth of real imports (because of a decline in oil imports). In addition, the exchange value of the dollar has increased moderately since mid-2011, reversing an overall downward trend since 2009 and making U.S. goods less price-competitive in foreign markets.

The Labor Market

The labor market experienced modest gains last year, but a substantial amount of slack remains in that market: According to CBO's estimates, employment in the fourth quarter of 2012 was more than 61/2 million less than it would have been if the economy had been operating at its maximum sustainable level.

The unemployment rate fell from 8.7 percent in the last quarter of 2011 to 7.8 percent in the last quarter of 2012. About 0.2 percentage points of that decline can be attributed to real GDP growth that was slightly faster than the growth of potential GDP during 2011 and 2012. (A reduction in the gap between actual and potential GDP tends to reduce the unemployment rate, although that reduction usually occurs with some delay and is spread over several quarters.) Much of the remainder of that decline probably reflects an unwinding of the factors that caused the especially large increases in unemployment that occurred in 2008 and 2009, when firms reduced employment by more than would have been expected on the basis of the decline in GDP. Those factors include fears of an even deeper recession than actually occurred and the effects of restricted availability of credit.[5]

In CBO's view, about 1 percentage point of the net rise of 2.8 percentage points in the unemployment rate that occurred between December 2007 (the peak of the previous economic expansion) and December 2012 reflects structural factors—such as mismatches between employers and employees and the erosion of workers' skills—that are associated with the recession but that are not directly linked to current aggregate demand. Such structural factors have contributed to the historically high share of unemployment accounted for by the long-term unemployed, people who have been seeking work for more than 26 consecutive weeks.[6] That share has topped 40 percent for the past three years (see Figure 2-3), far higher than in any other three-year period since World War II. CBO expects that share to remain high for the next few years.

The unemployment rate during the past several years would have been even higher if participation in the labor force had not declined so much over that period. (The rate of participation in the labor force describes the share of the civilian noninstitutionalized population age 16 or older that is either working or actively seeking work.) Participation fell from 66.0 percent in 2007 to 63.7 percent in 2012, an unusually large decrease over such a short period. About 1.3 percentage points of that decrease reflects the movement of the baby-boom generation into retirement (the oldest members of that group turned 65 in 2011), and about 0.3 percentage points can be directly attributed to the elevated rate of unemployment. The factors contributing to the remaining 0.7 percentage points are unclear but may include an unusually large response to the protracted weakness in the labor market.

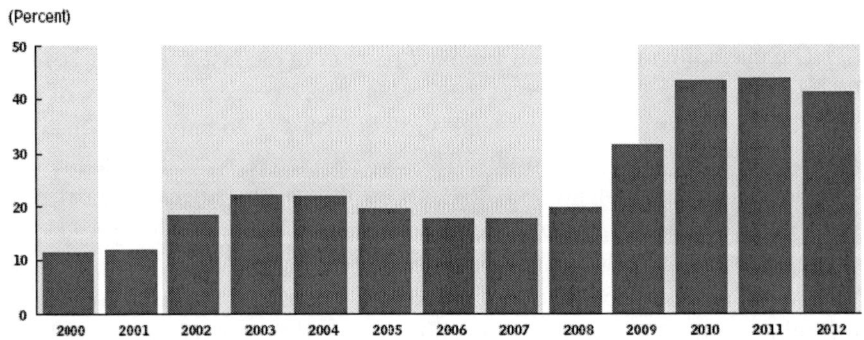

Sources: Congressional Budget Office; Department of Labor, Bureau of Labor Statistics.

Notes: Data show the percentage of unemployed U.S. workers who have been unemployed for longer than 26 consecutive weeks. Data are annual and are plotted through 2012.

Figure 2-3. Long-Term Unemployment.

The growth of labor compensation (the combination of wages and benefits that workers receive) picked up a bit in 2012 but continued to be restrained by the weak demand for labor. Real labor compensation grew by 1.6 percent in 2012, in CBO's estimation, mostly from increases in the number of workers; real labor compensation per worker grew by only 0.2 percent. Because of the tepid growth of employment and wages in recent years, total real labor compensation at the end of 2012 was slightly below its value in late 2007, just before the start of the recent recession.

Inflation and Interest Rates

Inflation moderated in 2012, and interest rates remained low. By CBO's estimates, consumer prices, measured by the price index for personal consumption expenditures, increased by 1.5 percent last year (as measured on a fourth-quarter-to-fourth-quarter basis), compared with an increase of 2.5 percent in 2011. That moderation is largely attributable to smaller increases in prices for gasoline and food. The core PCE price index—which excludes food and energy prices—also increased by 1.5 percent in 2012, down a little from 1.7 percent in 2011.[7] Other measures, the consumer price index for all urban consumers (CPI-U) and its core version, increased by 1.9 percent last year. (Rates for the CPI-U differ from those for the PCE price index because of the methods used to calculate those indexes and the larger role of housing rents in the CPI-U.) Since the recession began in December 2007, overall inflation has averaged 1.7 percent a year according to the PCE price index and 1.9 percent according to the CPI-U.

Interest rates remained low in 2012. Short-term interest rates were near zero, and longer-term rates declined to extremely low levels in the first half of 2012 and stayed unusually low thereafter. Those low rates reflect several factors:

- Investors' expectations that U.S. output will be below its potential for a few years;
- Investors' concerns about banking and fiscal problems in Europe; and
- Ongoing efforts by monetary policymakers to keep short- and long-term interest rates low, using the traditional and nontraditional policy actions employed since the recession.

That last factor includes the Federal Reserve's announcement in late 2012 that it intends to keep its target for the federal funds rate (the interest rate on overnight lending among banks that the Federal Reserve adjusts to conduct monetary policy) near zero until labor market conditions improve or inflation rises notably, and to continue purchasing long-term Treasury securities and mortgage-backed securities.[8]

The Economic Outlook for 2013 to 2018

CBO's economic outlook builds on the indications of a strengthening economy in 2012, but CBO expects that real GDP will grow slowly in 2013 because of fiscal tightening by the federal government that is scheduled to occur under current law. The agency's projections show the economy growing more strongly after this year and returning to its potential level in 2017. The anticipated improvement in the economy over the next few years reflects the fading effects of the housing and financial crisis, which have held down spending on housing, consumer goods and services, and business structures, equipment, and software. If some or all of the fiscal tightening scheduled to occur under current law was removed, the additional federal spending, lower tax revenues, or both would cause output to be greater and unemployment lower in the next few years than CBO projects. However, unless sufficient additional tightening was imposed later, output and income would be restrained in the middle of the coming decade and beyond by higher federal debt.

The Economic Outlook for 2013

Under current law, real GDP will increase by 1.4 percent in 2013 after growing by an estimated 1.9 percent in 2012, CBO projects (see Figure 2-4 and Table 2-1). Consistent with that slow growth, the unemployment rate is expected to edge up from its 7.8 percent reading at the end of last year to 8.0 percent in the fourth quarter of this year. The rate of inflation (as measured by the PCE price index) is estimated to decline to 1.3 percent this year (compared with 1.5 percent in 2012), largely as a consequence of declining energy prices. In CBO's forecast, interest rates stay very low this year; the rate on 3-month Treasury bills hovers near zero, and the rate on 10-year Treasury notes remains under 21/2 percent. Economic growth is projected to slow in 2013 primarily because of federal fiscal tightening. Federal spending on goods and services drops significantly in CBO's projections, primarily as a result of the automatic spending reductions specified in current law. (Those reductions were slated to begin in January of this year but were delayed until March by the American Taxpayer Relief Act.) Changes in tax rules are also expected to curtail growth in 2013. The 2 percentage-point cut in the payroll tax that first went into effect in January 2011 expired in January 2013, as did some reductions in tax rates originally enacted in the Economic Growth and Tax Relief Reconciliation Act of 2001 (P.L. 107-16) and the Jobs and Growth Tax Relief Reconciliation Act of 2003 (P.L. 108-27). Those changes will reduce after-tax income for many people, which will constrain the growth of consumer spending. That slowdown, in turn, will restrain overall growth in output and employment this year.

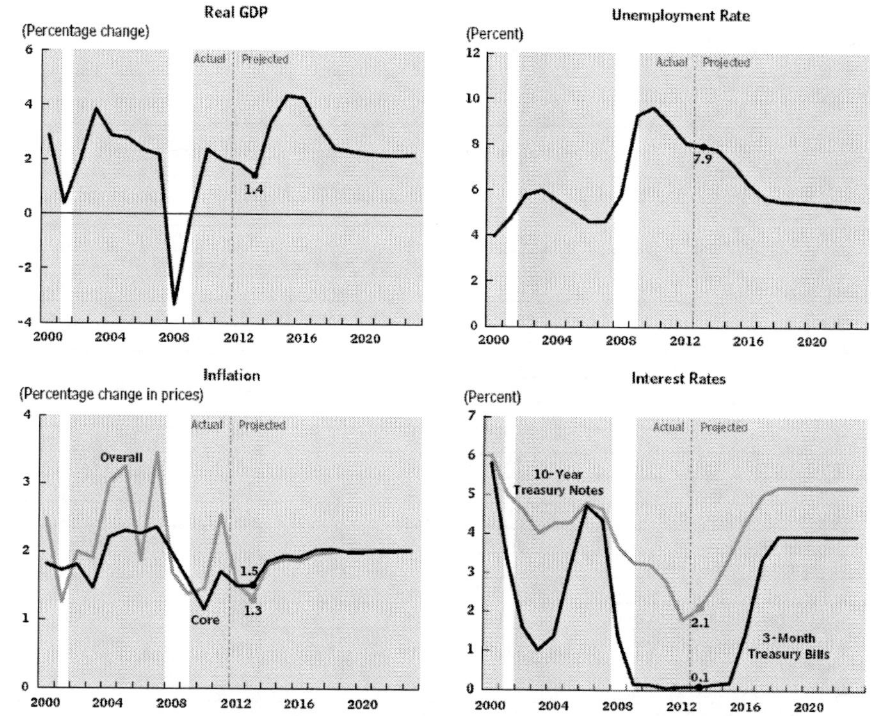

Sources: Congressional Budget Office; Department of Commerce, Bureau of Economic Analysis; Department of Labor, Bureau of Labor Statistics; Federal Reserve.

Notes: Real gross domestic product (GDP) is the output of the economy adjusted to remove the effects of inflation.

The unemployment rate is a measure of the number of jobless people who are available for work and are actively seeking jobs, expressed as a percentage of the labor force.

The overall inflation rate is based on the price index for personal consumption expenditures; the core rate excludes prices for food and energy.

Data are annual and are plotted through 2023. Forecast values for 2013 are labeled.

For real GDP and inflation, actual data are plotted through 2011; the values for 2012 reflect CBO's estimates for the fourth quarter and do not incorporate data recently released by the Department of Commerce and the Department of Labor. Percentage changes are measured between the fourth quarters of successive years.

For the unemployment rate and interest rates, actual data are plotted through 2012.

Figure 2.4. Actual Values and CBO's Projections of Key Economic Indicators.

Table 2-1. CBO's Economic Projections for Calendar Years 2012 to 2023

	Estimated, 2012	Forecast 2013	2014	Projected Annual Average 2015–2018	2019-2023
Gross Domestic Product		**Fourth Quarter to Fourth Quarter (Percentage change)**			
Real	1.9	1.4	3.4	3.6	2.2
Nominal	3.7	2.9	5.3	5.7	4.3
Inflation					
PCE price index	1.5	1.3	1.8	1.9	2.0
Core PCE price index[a]	1.5	1.5	1.9	2.0	2.0
Consumer price index[b]	1.9 c	1.5	2.0	2.2	2.3
Core consumer price index[a]	1.9 c	1.8	2.0	2.2	2.3
GDP price index	1.8	1.5	1.9	2.1	2.0
Employment Cost Index[d]	1.9	2.2	3.3	4.0	3.6
		Fourth Quarter Level (Percent)			
Unemployment Rate	7.8 c	8.0	7.6	5.5 e	5.2 f
		Year to Year (Percentage change)			
Gross Domestic Product					
Real	2.3	1.4	2.6	3.7	2.3
Nominal	4.1	2.9	4.4	5.9	4.3
Inflation					
PCE price index	1.7	1.3	1.7	1.9	2.0
Core PCE price index[a]	1.7	1.3	1.8	2.0	2.0
Consumer price index[b]	2.1 c	1.6	1.9	2.2	2.3
Core consumer price index[a]	2.1 c	1.7	2.0	2.2	2.3
GDP price index	1.8	1.5	1.8	2.1	2.0
Employment Cost Index[d]	1.8	2.1	2.9	4.0	3.6
	Calendar Year Average				
Unemployment Rate (Percent)	8.1 c	7.9	7.8	6.1	5.4
Payroll Employment (Monthly change, in thousands)	157 c	105	182	171	75
Interest Rates (Percent)					
Three-month Treasury bills	0.1 c	0.1	0.2	2.2	4.0
Ten-year Treasury notes	1.8 c	2.1	2.7	4.5	5.2
Tax Bases (Percentage of GDP)					
Wages and salaries	44.1	43.5	43.9	44.2	44.9
Domestic economic profits	9.6	9.3	9.7	9.7	7.7

Source: Congressional Budget Office. (Actual values for 2012 are from Department of Labor, Bureau of Labor Statistics; Federal Reserve.) Notes: Economic projections for each year from 2012 to 2023 appear in Appendix B.

The numbers shown here do not reflect the values for GDP and related series released by the Commerce Department's Bureau of Economic Analysis on January 30 and the values released by the Labor Department's Bureau of Labor Statistics for the employment cost index on January 31 and for payroll employment on February 1.

PCE = personal consumption expenditures; GDP = gross domestic product.

[a] Excludes prices for food and energy.

[b] The consumer price index for all urban consumers.

[c] Actual value for 2012.

[d] The employment cost index for wages and salaries of workers in private industry.

[e] Value for 2018.

[f] Value for 2023.

If all of the fiscal tightening still embodied in current law for 2013 was removed, growth in real GDP would be about 11/2 percentage points higher this year than CBO currently projects.[9] About 11/4 percentage points of that effect comes from the automatic reductions in federal spending described in Section 1, the expiration of the cut in payroll tax rates, and the increase in marginal tax rates on higher income; the spending changes and the combined tax changes account for about equal portions. (The spending changes have a smaller budgetary impact than the tax changes, but they affect GDP by a larger amount per dollar of budgetary cost.) The remaining 1/4 percentage point comes from other, smaller changes in spending and taxes. Even if all of the scheduled fiscal tightening in 2013 was removed, the economy would remain below its potential level and the unemployment rate would remain high for some time, CBO estimates. Gathering strength in some sectors will keep the economy growing despite the impending fiscal tightening, CBO projects. For example, residential investment is expected to continue to improve, and increases in house prices and stock prices will boost households' wealth. CBO anticipates that consumer spending will grow moderately, increasing aggregate demand. As a result, business investment will rise, helping to spur additional hiring and further bolstering the wealth of households. Continued easing of credit conditions will also support spending by households and businesses.

The Economic Outlook for 2014 to 2018

The growth of real GDP will pick up considerably beginning in 2014, CBO projects, after economic activity adjusts to this year's fiscal tightening. In CBO's projections, economic growth is 3.4 percent in 2014 and averages 3.6 percent per year in 2015 through 2018 (see Table 2-1). That growth closes the gap between actual and potential GDP by 2017. As a result of that stronger economic growth, the unemployment rate in CBO's forecast falls from 8.0 percent in the fourth quarter of 2013 to 6.8 percent in the fourth quarter of 2015 and then declines gradually to 5.5 percent in the fourth quarter of 2018.

The quickening of economic growth in 2014 reflects CBO's projections of continued improvements in households' income and wealth and in credit markets. Consumer spending will be supported by faster growth in wages and salaries (a result of more robust employment growth) and by continued gains in household wealth, owing to persistent increases in house prices and stock prices. Stronger demand for goods and services by households, in turn, will encourage businesses to undertake investments in structures and equipment as well as to engage in further hiring. Greater availability of credit will also support consumer spending and business investment. In addition, CBO expects that increased spending by federal, state, and local governments will add a small amount to overall demand after 2013. In contrast, net exports are likely to decline for much of the 2014–2018 period while growth in the United States outpaces growth among its major trading partners. From 2014 through 2018, CBO projects, the rate of inflation as measured by the PCE price index and its corresponding core index will rise slowly and then remain at 2 percent. CBO expects the CPI-U and its core version to increase a little more rapidly than their PCE counterparts. As economic growth and financial markets improve domestically and abroad, CBO anticipates, short-term and long-term interest rates will rise. In CBO's forecast, monetary policymakers begin raising the federal funds rate in early 2016 and selling assets from the Federal Reserve's securities portfolio later in that year. In addition, CBO projects that as the effects of the financial crisis and recession fade, and as economies in Europe improve, demand for risk-free U.S. Treasury securities will decline to a more normal level as demand for other assets increases. Finally, an improvement in economic growth will raise the demand for credit, putting upward pressure on interest rates more broadly. All told, the interest rate on 3-month Treasury bills in CBO's projection climbs from 0.1 percent in the fourth quarter of 2013 to 4.0 percent in the fourth quarter of 2018 (see Figure 2-4). Over the same period, the rate on 10-year Treasury notes is projected to increase from 2.3 percent to 5.2 percent.

Some Uncertainties in the Economic Outlook

Economic forecasts are always uncertain, but the uncertainty surrounding CBO's forecast for the next several years is especially great because the current business cycle has been unusual in a variety of ways.[10] Following the agency's usual practice, CBO constructed its forecast to lie in the middle of the distribution of possible outcomes for the economy given the fiscal policies that are embodied in current law. Even if no significant changes are made to fiscal policy, actual outcomes will undoubtedly differ from CBO's economic projections for various reasons. For example, the economy could grow considerably faster than CBO has forecast if exports are stronger as a result of more robust economic growth abroad than the agency has projected. Such an increase in exports could then speed the growth of employment and boost U.S. businesses' spending on structures, equipment, and software, potentially leading to a self-reinforcing cycle of increased spending, hiring, and income generation. Outcomes that are worse than those in CBO's forecast also are possible, however. For instance, if spending by businesses failed to improve after 2013 (perhaps because of an increase in uncertainty or tightening in the availability of credit owing to disruptions in financial markets), then investment and hiring could remain weak. That outcome could trigger a downturn in consumer spending and stall the recovery in the housing market, which could, in turn, reinforce the weakness in investment and hiring by businesses.

The Economic Outlook for 2019 to 2023

For the second half of the coming decade, CBO does not attempt to predict cyclical ups and downs of the economy but assumes instead that real GDP will equal its maximum sustainable level. Thus, CBO's assessment of the outlook for output and income for 2019 to 2023 depends on projections of trends in the factors of production that underlie potential output: the size of the labor force, the stock of productive capital, and the productivity of those factors. CBO's projections of those trends reflect the negative effects of the recession of 2007–2009 and the ensuing slow recovery as well as the impact of fiscal policy under current law. The projections through 2023 further reflect the expectation that the Federal Reserve will keep inflation low and stable.

Potential Output

Potential GDP is projected to grow at an average annual rate of 2.3 percent between 2019 and 2023, substantially below the average rate since 1950 of 3.3 percent (see Table 2-2). That estimate is mainly a result of slower projected growth in the potential labor force (the labor force adjusted for variations caused by the business cycle). That growth is expected to decline from its 1.5 percent average annual rate since 1950 to a 0.5 percent average annual rate during the coming decade, mostly owing to the retirement of the baby-boom generation and an end to the long-standing increase in the labor force participation of women.[11] For the nonfarm business sector, which makes up the bulk of the economy, CBO also expects the growth of capital services (the flow of services available from the stock of capital assets, such as equipment and structures) to be slower over the coming decade than it has been, on average, since 1950, primarily reflecting the slower growth of the labor force but also greater federal borrowing as a share of GDP. Similarly, CBO anticipates that the growth of potential total factor productivity (the potential efficiency in producing goods and services— specifically, the average real output per unit of input from labor and capital services combined, adjusted for variations caused by the business cycle) will be slower as well.

CBO's projections for growth of all three factors that underlie potential output have been dampened by the recent recession and the ensuing slow recovery. In particular, CBO estimates the following:

- Persistent long-term unemployment will lead some workers to leave the workforce earlier than they would have otherwise and will erode the skills of other workers, making it harder for them to find work in the coming years;
- The cumulative effect of the projected rebound in investment over the next decade will not entirely make up for the investment lost during the recession; and
- Growth in total factor productivity has been held down as the recession and slow recovery have delayed the reallocation of workers to their most productive uses, slowed the rate at which workers gain new skills as technologies evolve, and lowered spending by businesses on research and development.

  Combining those effects, CBO estimates that potential output will be about 11/2 percent lower in 2023 than it would have been without the recession and slow recovery; each of the three factors accounts for about one-third of the reduction.[12]

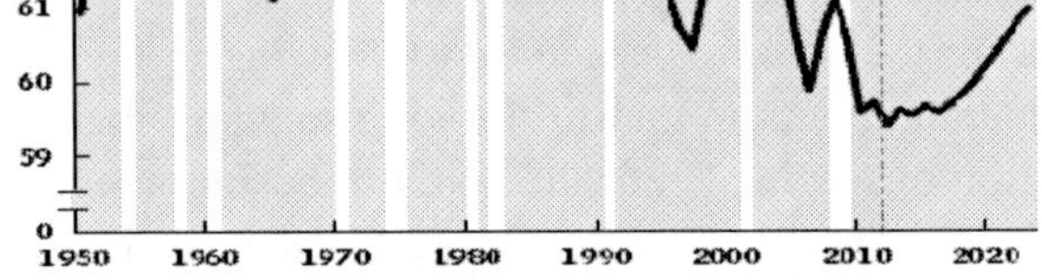

Sources: Congressional Budget Office; Department of Commerce, Bureau of Economic Analysis.

Notes: Labor income is defined as the sum of the compensation of employees and CBO's estimate of the labor share of proprietors' income. Gross domestic income is the sum of all income earned in the production of gross domestic product.

Data are annual. Actual data are plotted through 2011. The value for 2012 reflects CBO's estimate for the fourth quarter. Projections are plotted through 2023.

Figure 2-5. Labor Income.

Table 2-2. Key Assumptions in CBO's Projection of Potential GDP (By calendar year, in percent)

	Average Annual Growth						Projected Average Annual Growth		
	1950-1973	1974-1981	1982-1990	1991-2001	2002-2012	Total, 1950-2012	2013-2018	2019-2023	Total, 2013-2023
	Overall Economy								
Potential GDP	3.9	3.3	3.1	3.1	2.2	3.3	2.2	2.3	2.2
Potential Labor Force	1.6	2.5	1.6	1.3	0.8	1.5	0.6	0.5	0.5
Potential Labor Productivity[a]	2.3	0.8	1.5	1.8	1.4	1.7	1.6	1.8	1.7
	Nonfarm Business Sector								
Potential GDP	4.0	3.6	3.2	3.5	2.5	3.5	2.6	2.6	2.6
Potential Hours Worked	1.4	2.4	1.6	1.2	0.5	1.3	0.5	0.5	0.5
Capital Services	3.8	4.3	4.1	4.7	2.3	3.8	3.3	3.3	3.3
Potential TFP	1.9	0.7	0.9	1.3	1.4	1.4	1.2	1.3	1.3
Potential TFP excluding adjustments	1.9	0.7	0.9	1.2	1.3	1.4	1.3	1.3	1.3
Adjustments to TFP (Percentage points)[b]	0	0	0	0.1	0.2	*	**	0	**
Contributions to the Growth of									
Potential GDP (Percentage points)									
Potential hours worked	0.9	1.7	1.1	0.8	0.3	0.9	0.3	0.4	0.3
Capital input	1.2	1.3	1.2	1.4	0.7	1.1	1.0	1.0	1.0
Potential TFP	1.9	0.7	0.9	1.3	1.4	1.4	1.2	1.3	1.3
Total Contributions	4.0	3.6	3.2	3.5	2.5	3.5	2.6	2.6	2.6
Potential Labor Productivity[c]	2.6	1.2	1.6	2.3	2.0	2.1	2.1	2.1	2.1

Source: Congressional Budget Office.

Notes: Potential GDP is the maximum sustainable level of output in the economy. GDP = gross domestic product; TFP = total factor productivity; * = between zero and 0.05 percentage points; ** = between -0.05 percentage points and zero.

[a] The ratio of potential GDP to the potential labor force.

[b] The adjustments reflect CBO's estimates of the effect of the unusually rapid growth of TFP between 2001 and 2003 and the effect of the 2007–2009 recession on potential TFP.

[c] The estimated trend in the ratio of potential GDP to potential hours worked in the nonfarm business sector.

Unemployment, Inflation, and Interest Rates

In CBO's projections, the unemployment rate inches down from 5.5 percent at the end of 2018 to 5.2 percent by 2023. That decline matches the decline over that same period in the agency's estimate of the natural rate of unemployment (the rate arising from all sources except fluctuations in aggregate demand). CBO expects that the difficulty the long-term unemployed face in finding jobs—for example, because of the erosion of their skills or because of employers' perception that their absence from the job market is an indication of their quality as workers—will gradually diminish but not completely disappear by 2023; as a result, the natural rate of unemployment edges downward during the 2019–2023 period in CBO's projection. Both inflation and core inflation as measured by the PCE price index are forecast to stay at 2.0 percent in the period from 2019 to 2023, in line with the Federal Reserve's announced target for inflation. (Average inflation as measured by the CPI-U is projected to be slightly higher.) CBO forecasts that the interest rates on 3-month Treasury bills and 10-year Treasury notes will average 4.0 percent and 5.2 percent, respectively, for the period. Those rates are consistent with the historical relationships among interest rates, inflation, federal borrowing, and the factors that underlie the growth of potential GDP. In particular, the rate on 10-year Treasury notes adjusted for inflation is projected to equal about 3 percent from 2019 to 2023, higher than its long-run historical average primarily because CBO forecasts a higher-than-average ratio of federal debt to GDP during that period.

Projections of Income

Economic activity and federal tax revenues depend not only on the amount of total income in the economy but also on how that income is divided among its constituent parts: wages and salaries, domestic economic profits, proprietors' income, interest and dividend income, and other categories. CBO forecasts various categories of income by projecting their shares of total gross domestic income (GDI). (In principle, GDI equals GDP because the costs of production are tracked as income; in practice, they differ because of difficulties in measuring both quantities.) Labor income has fallen as a share of GDI during the economic recovery, continuing its previous downward trend (see Figure 2-5).[13] CBO estimates that labor's share averaged 59.4 percent in the fourth quarter of 2012, down from 61.0 percent in the second quarter of 2009 (at the end of the recession). Much of that weakness can be attributed to slower growth during the past few years in wages and salaries (the largest component of labor income) relative to growth in the other components of GDI. Historically, labor's share of income tends to decline early in recoveries and rise later. In CBO's projections, labor income grows faster than GDI over the next decade, bringing its share to 61.0 percent in 2023—still below its average of about 611/2 percent in recent decades. That increase stems from faster growth in real hourly labor compensation, which picks up during the first half of the projection period in response to stronger demand for labor and then remains strong during the latter years of the period, when it is assumed to match the growth of labor productivity and cause growth in labor income to exceed the growth of other types of income. Domestic economic profits, CBO estimates, were 9.7 percent of GDI in 2012 and will decline slightly as a share of GDI in 2013 as the economy slows a bit.[14] CBO expects that profits' share will then rise through 2016 before falling again thereafter—to about 7.3 percent in 2023—because of the rising burden of corporate interest payments, depreciation on the larger stock of business capital, and growth in labor income.

Comparison with Other Economic Projections

CBO's current economic forecast differs in some important respects from the forecast it issued in August 2012. The forecast also differs in various ways from the *Blue Chip* consensus forecast published in January and from the Federal Reserve's forecasts presented at the December 2012 meeting of the Federal Open Market Committee. CBO's current forecast for the growth of output in 2013 (1.4 percent) is significantly higher than its forecast from last August, when the agency projected that real GDP would decline by 0.5 percent (see Table 2-3). The August forecast was heavily influenced by the sharp fiscal tightening that had been scheduled to take effect in January 2013. However, the American Taxpayer Relief Act removed part of that fiscal tightening, boosting projected growth in real GDP in 2013 by between 11/2 and 13/4 percentage points. That effect, along with better-than-expected news about the economy, led CBO to revise upward its projected growth rate for real GDP this year. In contrast, CBO has revised downward its projection of the level of potential GDP in 2022, the last year of CBO's previous projections, by roughly 0.5 percent. That change primarily reflects data revisions that reduced historical estimates of capital services and, in turn, CBO's projection of those services. In addition, CBO estimates that greater federal borrowing under current law relative to the path in CBO's previous projections would reduce the size of the capital stock. That reduction would occur because, by CBO's estimates, federal borrowing would take up a larger share of the saving potentially available for private investment. Consistent with that greater federal borrowing and smaller capital stock, CBO raised its projection of the interest rate on 10-year Treasury notes in the latter part of the projection period to 5.2 percent from 5.0 percent in the previous projection.

CBO forecasts a weaker economy in the near term—with lower GDP growth in 2013 and a higher rate of unemployment over the next few years—than is forecast by the *Blue Chip* consensus or the Federal Reserve (see Table 2-4). Those differences in forecasts probably result from a variety of factors, including the economic data available when the forecasts were completed, the models used by the forecasters, and varying assumptions about future federal taxes and spending. In particular, a number of other forecasters report that they expect lawmakers to postpone some of the remaining near-term fiscal tightening, whereas CBO's forecast, based on current law, does not include such expectations.

Table 2-3. Comparison of CBO's Current and Previous Economic Projections for Calendar Years 2012 to 2022

	Estimated,		Forecast	Projected Annual Average	
	2012	2013	2014	2015–2018	2019–2022
Real GDP	**Fourth Quarter to Fourth Quarter (Percentage change)**				
February 2013	1.9	1.4	3.4	3.6	2.2
August 2012	2.1	-0.5	4.4	3.9	2.3
Nominal GDP					
February 2013	3.7	2.9	5.3	5.7	4.3
August 2012	3.9	0.8	6.0	5.9	4.4
PCE Price Index					
February 2013	1.5	1.3	1.8	1.9	2.0
August 2012	1.4	1.4	1.7	1.9	2.0
Consumer Price Index[a]					
February 2013	1.9 b	1.5	2.0	2.2	2.3
August 2012	1.3	1.6	1.9	2.2	2.3
GDP Price Index					
February 2013	1.8	1.5	1.9	2.1	2.0
August 2012	1.8	1.4	1.6	1.9	2.0
Employment Cost Index[c]					
February 2013	1.9	2.2	3.3	4.0	3.6
August 2012	2.6	2.4	3.4	4.4	3.7
Real Potential GDP					
February 2013	1.7	1.8	2.0	2.4	2.2
August 2012	1.7	1.6	1.9	2.4	2.3
	Calendar Year Average				
Unemployment Rate (Percent)					
February 2013	8.1[b]	7.9	7.8	6.1	5.4

	Estimated, 2012	2013	Forecast 2014	Projected Annual Average 2015–2018	2019–2022
August 2012	8.2	8.8	8.7	6.5	5.4
Interest Rates (Percent)					
Three-month Treasury bills					
February 2013	0.1 [b]	0.1	0.2	2.2	4.0
August 2012	0.1	0.1	0.2	2.2	3.8
Ten-year Treasury notes					
February 2013	1.8 [b]	2.1	2.7	4.5	5.2
August 2012	1.8	1.8	2.4	4.0	5.0
Tax Bases (Percentage of GDP)					
Wages and salaries					
February 2013	44.1	43.5	43.9	44.2	44.9
August 2012	44.1	44.0	44.1	44.7	45.4
Domestic economic profits					
February 2013	9.6	9.3	9.7	9.7	7.9
August 2012	10.4	9.0	9.4	9.3	7.6

Source: Congressional Budget Office. (Actual values for 2012 are from Department of Labor, Bureau of Labor Statistics; Federal Reserve.)

Notes: Estimated values do not reflect the values for GDP and related series released by the Commerce Department's Bureau of Economic Analysis on January 30 and the values for the employment cost index released by the Labor Department's Bureau of Labor Statistics on January 31.

GDP = gross domestic product; PCE = personal consumption expenditures.

[a] The consumer price index for all urban consumers.

[b] Actual value for 2012.

[c] The employment cost index for wages and salaries of workers in private industry.

Table 2-4. Comparison of Economic Projections by CBO, the *Blue Chip* Consensus, and the Federal Reserve (By calendar year)

	Estimated, 2012	2013	2014	2015	Longer Run[a]
	Fourth Quarter to Fourth Quarter (Percentage Change)				
Real GDP					
CBO	1.9	1.4	3.4	4.4	2.2
Blue Chip	1.9	2.2	2.8	n.a.	n.a.
Federal Reserve					
Range	1.6 to 2.0	2.0 to 3.2	2.8 to 4.0	2.5 to 4.2	2.2 to 3.0
Central tendency	1.7 to 1.8	2.3 to 3.0	3.0 to 3.5	3.0 to 3.7	2.3 to 2.5
PCE Price Index					
CBO	1.5	1.3	1.8	1.9	2.0

Table 2-4. (Continued)

	Estimated, 2012	2013	2014	2015	Longer Run[a]
	Fourth Quarter to Fourth Quarter (Percentage Change)				
Federal Reserve					
Range	1.6 to 1.8	1.3 to 2.0	1.4 to 2.2	1.5 to 2.2	2.0
Central tendency	1.6 to 1.7	1.3 to 2.0	1.5 to 2.0	1.7 to 2.0	2.0
Core PCE Price Index[b]					
CBO	1.5	1.5	1.9	1.9	2.0
Federal Reserve					
Range	1.6 to 1.8	1.5 to 2.0	1.5 to 2.0	1.7 to 2.2	n.a.
Central tendency	1.6 to 1.7	1.6 to 1.9	1.6 to 2.0	1.8 to 2.0	n.a.
Consumer Price Index[c]					
CBO	1.9[d]	1.5	2.0	2.1	2.3
Blue Chip	1.9	1.9	2.2	n.a.	n.a.
GDP Price Index					
CBO	1.8	1.5	1.9	2.1	2.0
Blue Chip	2.0	1.8	2.0	n.a.	n.a.
		Fourth Quarter Level (Percent)			
Unemployment Rate					
CBO	7.8[d]	8.0	7.6	6.8	5.2
Blue Chip	7.8[d]	7.5	7.0	n.a.	n.a.
Federal Reserve					
Range	7.7 to 8.0	6.9 to 7.8	6.1 to 7.4	5.7 to 6.8	5.0 to 6.0
Central tendency	7.8 to 7.9	7.4 to 7.7	6.8 to 7.3	6.0 to 6.6	5.2 to 6.0
Interest Rates					
Three-month Treasury bills					
CBO	0.1[d]	0.1	0.2	0.3	4.0
Blue Chip	0.1[d]	0.1	0.3	n.a.	n.a.
Ten-year Treasury notes					
CBO	1.7[d]	2.3	2.9	3.8	5.2
Blue Chip	1.7[d]	2.2	2.7	n.a.	n.a.

Sources: Congressional Budget Office; Aspen Publishers, *Blue Chip Economic Indicators* (January 10, 2013); Board of Governors of the Federal Reserve System, "Economic Projections of Federal Reserve Board Members and Federal Reserve Bank Presidents, December 2012" (December 12, 2012), www.federalreserve.gov/monetarypolicy/files /fomcprojtabl20121212.pdf; Department of Labor, Bureau of Labor Statistics; Federal Reserve.

Notes: The *Blue Chip* consensus is the average of about 50 forecasts by private-sector economists. The range of estimates from the Federal Reserve reflects the forecasts of the members of the Board of Governors and the presidents of the Federal Reserve Banks. The central tendency is that range without the three highest and three lowest projections. The *Blue Chip* consensus does not provide forecasts of the PCE or core PCE price indexes. The Federal Reserve does not provide forecasts of the consumer price index, the GDP price index, or interest rates. Estimated values for GDP and related series do not reflect the values for the fourth quarter of 2012 released by the Commerce Department's Bureau of Economic Analysis on January 30. GDP = gross domestic product; n.a. = not applicable; PCE = personal consumption expenditures.

[a] For CBO, values are for 2023. For the Federal Reserve, values represent assessments of the rate to which each variable would be expected to converge under appropriate monetary policy and in the absence of further shocks to the economy.

[b] Excludes prices for food and energy.

[c] The consumer price index for all urban consumers.

[d] Actual value for 2012.

APPENDIX A: CHANGES IN CBO'S BASELINE SINCE AUGUST 2012

The Congressional Budget Office (CBO) anticipates that in the absence of further legislation affecting spending and revenues, the deficit for 2013 will be $845 billion, or $204 billion more than the agency projected in August, when it released its previous set of baseline budgetary projections (see Table A-1).[1] CBO now estimates that the cumulative deficit over the 2013– 2022 period, under current law, will be $6.8 trillion, which is $4.6 trillion more than it projected in August. The enactment of legislation, most notably the American Taxpayer Relief Act of 2012 (Public Law 112-240), boosted the cumulative deficit by an estimated $4.7 trillion; together, changes in the economic outlook and other, technical, changes offset $129 billion of that increase. (For a description of the American Taxpayer Relief Act, see Box 1-1 in Section 1.)

For 2013, CBO estimates, revenues will be $204 billion less and outlays $1 billion lower than it had previously projected. Enactment of the American Taxpayer Relief Act will reduce revenues by an estimated $280 billion; that reduction is partially offset by increases in projected revenues because of economic and technical changes. The small drop in estimated outlays for the current year is the net result of nearly offsetting changes: reductions for technical reasons in CBO's estimates of both discretionary and mandatory spending ($58 billion), mostly offset by an estimated increase in mandatory outlays resulting from recent legislation ($41 billion), and other, smaller increases ($16 billion). For the 2013–2022 period, the change in deficits is dominated by a projected reduction in individual income tax receipts stemming from provisions in the American Taxpayer Relief Act; by itself, that reduction results in a projected increase of $3.2 trillion in the cumulative deficit over the 10-year period (excluding added debt-service costs). In all, revenues for that period are now projected to be about 9 percent less and outlays are projected to be about 2 percent less than the amounts CBO projected in August 2012. The changes in CBO's baseline include updates to the agency's projections of the budgetary effects of provisions in the Affordable Care Act that involve health insurance coverage.[2] Although several components of its estimates have changed since August, the difference in the net budgetary impact for the 2013–2022 period is less than $500 million.

Legislative Changes

Legislation enacted since the agency prepared its August baseline has had a substantial impact on CBO's estimates of revenues and outlays. By itself, the American Taxpayer Relief Act boosted projected deficits by $4.0 trillion, excluding debt-service costs (see Box 1-1 in Section 1). As a result of that and other new laws, CBO has increased its estimate of the deficit by $331 billion for 2013 and by $4.7 trillion (including debt service) for the 2013–2022 period.

Changes to Projections of Revenues

Because of the American Taxpayer Relief Act (and other legislation that will have much smaller effects on the budget), CBO has significantly reduced its projections of revenues for the next decade. Specifically, the agency lowered its projections of revenues by $280 billion for 2013 and by an additional $3.4 trillion for the 2014– 2022 period, which is in accord with estimates made by the staff of the Joint Committee on Taxation (JCT). (The act also will result in a $0.3 trillion increase in outlays for refundable tax credits, according to JCT's estimates.) The act's most significant effects appear in receipts from individual income taxes: CBO reduced its projection for those revenues by $224 billion for 2013 and by $3.2 trillion for the 2013–2022 period. The law permanently extended several revenue-reducing provisions that had been set to expire on December 31, 2012. Most of those provisions were originally enacted in the Economic Growth and Tax Relief Reconciliation Act of 2001 and the Jobs and Growth Tax Relief Reconciliation Act of 2003 and were then extended for two years in December 2010. (The American Taxpayer Relief Act did not extend several expiring tax provisions that applied to the income of high-income taxpayers, however.) The law also will reduce revenues from individual income taxes because it permanently extended the higher exemption amounts for the alternative minimum tax, which had expired, and indexed them for inflation.

Table A-1. Changes in CBO's Baseline Projections of the Deficit Since August 2012 (Billions of dollars)

											Total	
	2013	2014	2015	2016	2017	2018	2019	2020	2021	2022	2013-2017	2013-2022
Deficit in CBO's August 2012 Baseline	**-641**	**-387**	**-213**	**-186**	**-123**	**-79**	**-130**	**-142**	**-144**	**-213**	**-1,549**	**-2,258**
					Legislative Changes							
Changes in Revenues												
Individual income taxes	-224	-258	-254	-277	-304	-330	-351	-379	-410	-443	-1,317	-3,232
Corporate income taxes	-55	-15	9	5	4	2	*	-1	-2	-2	-52	-54
Social insurance taxes	*	-1	-1	-1	-1	-1	-1	-1	-1	-1	-2	-5
Other	*	-25	-30	-33	-36	-39	-42	-45	-48	-51	-124	-348
All Changes in Revenues	**-280**	**-299**	**-275**	**-305**	**-337**	**-367**	**-393**	**-426**	**-461**	**-497**	**-1,495**	**-3,639**
Changes in Outlays												
Mandatory												
Refundable tax credits	0	36	37	37	37	37	23	23	23	23	148	277
Unemployment compensation	22	8	0	0	0	0	0	0	0	0	30	30
Medicare	13	4	-3	-3	-3	*	*	-1	-1	-1	8	5
Other	5	0	0	2	4	1	*	*	*	-4	11	7
Subtotal	41	48	34	36	38	38	22	22	22	18	197	319
Discretionary	9	-8	-7	-3	2	5	7	9	10	11	-8	35
Debt service	1	5	7	20	42	73	96	122	153	185	75	704
All Changes in Outlays	**50**	**45**	**34**	**52**	**82**	**116**	**126**	**153**	**185**	**213**	**264**	**1,057**
Total Legislative Changes[a]	**-330**	**-344**	**-309**	**-358**	**-419**	**-483**	**-519**	**-579**	**-645**	**-710**	**-1,760**	**-4,696**
					Economic Changes							
Changes in Revenues												
Individual income taxes	20	32	34	29	24	10	*	-3	-4	*	139	142
Corporate income taxes	-13	-1	-5	*	9	12	11	10	7	2	-11	31
Social insurance taxes	4	6	*	-5	-9	-15	-19	-20	-19	-16	-5	-94

Table A-1. (Continued)

											Total	
	2013	2014	2015	2016	2017	2018	2019	2020	2021	2022	2013-2017	2013-2022
Other	1	3	2	-1	1	3	1	1	1	1	5	11
All Changes in Revenues	**13**	**39**	**30**	**22**	**24**	**9**	**-7**	**-13**	**-15**	**-13**	**128**	**90**
Changes in Outlays												
Mandatory												
Student loans	2	3	4	5	6	5	3	2	2	2	21	35
Social Security	4	4	4	5	4	2	1	*	-1	-3	20	19
Other	-4	-5	*	1	1	2	2	2	*	-2	-9	-5
Subtotal	2	2	8	11	10	9	6	3	1	-2	32	50
Discretionary	-1	*	*	*	-1	-1	-2	-2	-2	-2	-1	-11
Net interest												
Debt service	*	*	*	-1	-1	-1	*	2	4	5	-3	7
Other	*	7	8	8	14	31	31	30	28	28	37	186
Subtotal	*	7	8	7	13	30	31	32	32	33	34	192
All Changes in Outlays	**1**	**8**	**16**	**19**	**22**	**38**	**35**	**33**	**31**	**29**	**65**	**231**
Total Economic Changes[a]	**12**	**31**	**15**	**4**	**2**	**-29**	**-42**	**-46**	**-46**	**-42**	**63**	**-141**
					Technical Changes							
Changes in Revenues												
Individual income taxes	43	38	40	37	21	15	3	-2	-8	-14	179	172
Corporate income taxes	21	10	4	2	8	10	11	10	10	10	44	95
Social insurance taxes	-9	-3	-5	-8	-13	-16	-17	-19	-21	-25	-38	-136
Other	8	10	37	26	-21	-42	-48	-61	-47	-22	60	-160
All Changes in Revenues	**63**	**55**	**76**	**57**	**-5**	**-33**	**-50**	**-72**	**-67**	**-51**	**245**	**-29**
Changes in Outlays												
Mandatory												
Medicaid	-2	-9	-11	-10	-16	-24	-31	-38	-44	-52	-48	-236

											Total	
	2013	**2014**	**2015**	**2016**	**2017**	**2018**	**2019**	**2020**	**2021**	**2022**	**2013-2017**	**2013-2022**
Medicare	-6	-9	-9	-9	-10	-11	-15	-18	-22	-29	-42	-137
Veterans' compensation and pensions	5	8	9	12	12	11	13	13	12	13	45	108
Fannie Mae and Freddie Mac	-29	*	*	*	-1	-1	-1	-2	-3	-6	-30	-44
Other	1	-8	-1	-3	5	8	4	2	1	4	-6	13
Subtotal	-31	-19	-11	-10	-10	-18	-30	-43	-56	-69	-81	-296
Discretionary	-27	-15	-3	-8	-4	1	2	2	2	2	-56	-47
Net interest												
Debt service	*	1	6	4	-7	-17	-18	-23	-22	-17	5	-92
Other	5	3	7	8	10	14	15	24	27	25	32	137
Subtotal	5	4	13	12	3	-2	-3	1	5	7	37	45
All Changes in Outlays	**-52**	**-30**	**-1**	**-7**	**-10**	**-19**	**-31**	**-40**	**-49**	**-60**	**-100**	**-298**
Total Technical Changes[a]	**114**	**84**	**78**	**64**	**5**	**-14**	**-20**	**-32**	**-19**	**8**	**345**	**269**
						All Changes						
Total Effect on the Deficit[a]	**-204**	**-229**	**-217**	**-290**	**-412**	**-526**	**-580**	**-656**	**-710**	**-744**	**-1,352**	**-4,568**
Deficit in CBO's February 2013 Baseline	**-845**	**-616**	**-430**	**-476**	**-535**	**-605**	**-710**	**-798**	**-854**	**-957**	**-2,901**	**-6,825**
Memorandum:												
Effects on the Deficit[a]												
Changes in revenues	-204	-206	-168	-226	-318	-391	-450	-511	-543	-561	-1,122	-3,577
Changes in outlays	1	-23	-49	-64	-94	-135	-130	-146	-167	-183	-230	-990

Source: Congressional Budget Office.

Note: * = between -$500 million and $500 million.

a. Negative numbers indicate an increase in the deficit; positive numbers indicate a decrease in the deficit.

Furthermore, the American Taxpayer Relief Act modified laws concerning estate and gift taxes, extending most features that were in effect in 2012 but raising the top tax rate by 5 percentage points, to 40 percent. Because the top rate under prior law was scheduled to rise to 55 percent and the amount subject to taxes was scheduled to rise after 2012, CBO reduced its projections for revenues from estate and gift taxes by $348 billion for the next decade.

Legislation also caused CBO to lower its projection of revenues from corporate income taxes—by $54 billion for the 2013–2022 period; the largest change was for 2013. The effects stemmed mostly from a one-year extension of provisions that allow businesses to accelerate deductions for the cost of acquiring equipment and a two-year extension of a host of business tax credits and deductions.

Changes to Projections of Outlays

Since August, CBO has raised the amount it estimates for outlays in fiscal year 2013 by $51 billion because of legislative actions that are projected to boost mandatory outlays by $41 billion and discretionary outlays by $9 billion. For the 2013–2022 period, outlays are now projected to be higher by $1.0 trillion (or 2.4 percent), largely because of higher debt-service costs related to enacted legislation and increased outlays for refundable tax credits.

Mandatory Spending

CBO and JCT estimate that the American Taxpayer Relief Act will result in an increase of $309 billion in mandatory spending over the 2013–2022 period. (That total does not include the $24 billion cost of eliminating a portion of this year's automatic spending reductions; much of that effect is classified as discretionary spending in the baseline.) Most of that increase ($277 billion) is the result of additional payments for certain refundable tax credits (which are recorded in the budget as outlays). Among other provisions, the law also extended emergency unemployment compensation (which CBO estimates will boost outlays by $30 billion over the 2013–2014 period) and delayed by one year scheduled cuts in Medicare's payments to physicians (raising estimated outlays by $25 billion over the 10-year period); other changes to Medicare yielded estimated savings of $20 billion for that period.[3]

Discretionary Spending

Since August, CBO has increased its baseline projections of discretionary spending by $9 billion for 2013 and by $35 billion for the 2013–2022 period. Those increases arise mainly from the baseline's treatment of supplemental funding provided in response to Hurricane Sandy and of appropriations in 2013 for overseas contingency operations. In January, the Disaster Relief Appropriations Act, 2013 (P.L. 113-2), provided about $50 billion in discretionary budget authority for relief and recovery from Hurricane Sandy. Most of that amount, $41 billion, was designated as emergency spending and has been extrapolated fully in CBO's baseline. The law also provided $5 billion in funding designated for disaster relief (as defined in the Budget Control Act) and $3 billion that was not designated either as emergency funding or for disaster relief; both amounts are extrapolated in CBO's baseline but are subject to constraints imposed by the Budget Control Act in future years. Overall, the additional funding for 2013 and the extrapolation of those supplemental appropriations added about $330 billion to CBO's projections of discretionary outlays for the 2013–2022 period. As a result of the Continuing Appropriations Resolution, 2013 (P.L. 112-175), enacted in September 2012, funding for overseas contingency operations in 2013 is $27 billion less than the amount that had been projected in the previous baseline (that amount was equal to the 2012 appropriation, adjusted for inflation). Extrapolating that smaller amount of funding reduces the projection of outlays for the 2013–2022 period by $277 billion. The American Taxpayer Relief Act also altered the automatic enforcement procedures established in the Budget Control Act that require reductions in 2013 for discretionary and mandatory funding. The law delayed the procedures' implementation by two months and decreased the amount of the reduction required for 2013 by a total of $24 billion, most of it in the category of discretionary spending. That change boosted CBO's baseline projection of discretionary outlays by $22 billion for the 2013–2022 period. (That increase was offset by certain other changes to revenues and spending that were made by the act.) Other changes stemming from the amount of funding provided in the continuing resolution reduce discretionary outlays in the baseline by about $40 billion between 2013 and 2022.

Economic Changes

CBO's latest economic forecast incorporates updated projections of gross domestic product, the unemployment rate, interest rates, inflation, and other economic variables that affect federal outlays and revenues (see Section 2). Those updates have led CBO to trim its projection of the deficit for 2013 by $12 billion and to increase its projection of the cumulative deficit for the

2013–2022 period by $141 billion, mostly because of the increased cost of interest on the debt.

Changes to Projections of Revenues

Revisions to CBO's economic forecast caused the agency to increase its projections of revenues by $13 billion for 2013 and by $90 billion (or 0.2 percent) for the 2013– 2022 period. Compared with the projections released in August, revenues are now expected to be $138 billion greater for the first part of the projection period, from 2013 to 2018, but $47 billion lower for the 2019–2022 period. For the first half of the period, CBO increased its projections of personal income—including wages and salaries, interest income, and proprietors' income—in part because of the enactment of the American Taxpayer Relief Act and its removal of much of the fiscal tightening scheduled under prior law. All else being equal, those changes in income imply higher revenues from individual income taxes and social insurance taxes. The effects on social insurance revenues were largely offset, however, by an estimated reduction in receipts from state unemployment taxes (which are counted as federal revenues); CBO expects that larger balances in state unemployment trust funds will lead states to reduce their unemployment taxes.

CBO projects lower wages and salaries for the second half of the period, which would also reduce the amounts it anticipates in revenues from individual income and social insurance taxes. But the agency's estimates of receipts from individual income taxes have changed little since August because reductions in wages and salaries have been offset by increases in interest income and proprietors' income. CBO increased the amount it projects for receipts from corporate income taxes to reflect an anticipated increase in domestic corporate profits.

Changes to Projections of Outlays

Revisions to CBO's economic forecast have prompted the agency to increase its estimates of outlays (including debt service), boosting them by $1 billion for the current year and by $231 billion (or 0.5 percent) for the 2013–2022 period. The change for the 10-year period is mostly the result of higher projected interest rates.

Net Interest

Economic revisions to CBO's projections of spending for net interest have two components: the effects of changes in the agency's projections of interest rates and inflation and the effects on the government's borrowing that result from the impact of economic changes on revenues and noninterest outlays. Overall, CBO projects that changes in the economic forecast will result in outlays for net interest over the 2013–2022 period that are $192 billion higher than the amount it estimated in August. Almost all of that change stems from CBO's updated projections of interest rates and inflation, which in turn have resulted in estimates of net interest that are $186 billion higher than they were in August. CBO now expects higher interest rates for most securities throughout the 2013–2022 period. Upward revisions to interest rates for securities with a maturity of less than one year range from 1 basis point to 45 basis points for that period.[4] For securities with a maturity of two years or more, upward revisions range from 1 basis point to 58 basis points for the same period.

Mandatory Spending

Updates to its economic forecast caused CBO to raise its estimates of mandatory outlays for the current year by $2 billion and for the 2013–2022 period by $50 billion.

Student Loans

Consistent with the procedures set forth in the Federal Credit Reform Act of 1990, annual outlays for the student loan program represent the costs of the subsidies provided by the government. Those costs are measured as the present value of the future cash flows associated with new federal loans disbursed each year, calculated using the Department of the Treasury's borrowing rates to discount those cash flows.[5]

In updating its economic forecast, CBO raised its estimate of those rates for the 2013–2022 period. With higher discount rates, the estimated present value of future cash flows associated with student loans decreases (that is, such cash flows are discounted more). Because those future cash flows will be income to the government (in the form of loan repayments, interest payments, and default recoveries), CBO now anticipates that net outlays for student loans over the 2013–2022 period will be $35 billion higher than it projected in August. (On balance, CBO estimates that the student loan program produces net negative subsidies under the Federal Credit Reform Act's present-value methodology; the revised, higher discount rates produce lower estimates of net negative subsidies.)

Social Security

Because of changes in the economic forecast, CBO increased by $19 billion the amount it projects that the government will spend for Social Security over the 2013–2022 period. The cost-of-living adjustment of 1.7 percent that Social Security beneficiaries received in January 2013 is 0.6 percentage points higher than CBO anticipated in August. Projected cost-of-living adjustments for the 2014–2022 period are only slightly different from the amounts in the August forecast. Those changes boost the agency's estimates of benefit payments for the period by $39 billion. In contrast, revisions to CBO's projections of the growth in wages and salaries (which affect initial benefits) result in estimates of benefit amounts that are lower by about $20 billion between 2013 and 2022.

Technical Changes

Technical updates to CBO's estimates of revenues and outlays—that is, revisions that do not stem from legislation or changes in economic assumptions—have resulted in a net decrease of $115 billion in the estimated deficit for 2013 and a net decrease of $270 billion in the cumulative deficit for 2013 through 2022.

Changes to Projections of Outlays

As a result of technical revisions to CBO's projections, the agency has reduced its estimate of spending by $52 billion for 2013 and by $299 billion (or 0.7 percent) for the 2013–2022 period. CBO made nearly equal reductions in its estimates of discretionary and mandatory spending for the current year; in contrast, for the 2013–2022 period, most of the revision is in projections of outlays for mandatory programs (most notably for Medicaid, Medicare, and veterans' programs).

Mandatory Spending

Technical revisions related to mandatory programs have reduced the amounts projected for spending in the current year by $31 billion, primarily because of an increase in estimated receipts related to the Treasury's transactions with Fannie Mae and Freddie Mac. For the 2013–2022 period as a whole, technical adjustments, largely related to Medicaid and Medicare, reduce the net amount projected for mandatory spending by $297 billion.

Medicaid and Medicare

In recent years, health care spending has grown much more slowly both nationally and for federal programs than historical rates would have indicated. (For example, in 2012, federal spending for Medicare and Medicaid was about 5 percent below the amount that CBO had projected in March 2010.) In response to that slowdown, over the past several years, CBO has made a series of downward technical adjustments to its projections of spending for Medicaid and Medicare. From the March 2010 baseline to the current baseline, such technical revisions have lowered estimates of federal spending for the two programs in 2020 by about $200 billion—by $126 billion for Medicare and by $78 billion for Medicaid, or by roughly 15 percent for each program. Spending projections also have been affected by legislative action—most notably as a result of the Affordable Care Act—and by updated economic forecasts. From 2010 to the present, those other types of revisions boosted the estimates of outlays for Medicare and Medicaid in 2020 by $72 billion, or about 5 percent. (The Affordable Care Act also created new subsidies for some people to purchase health insurance through exchanges, adding $115 billion to the estimate for federal outlays for health care programs in 2020, according to CBO's current projections.) For the 2013–2022 period, technical changes to estimates for the Medicaid program have reduced projections for spending by $236 billion (or 5.5 percent) relative to CBO's estimates in August 2012. (Changes to estimates of Medicaid outlays related to legislation or economic factors amounted only to $3 billion.) The revisions reflect both lower anticipated enrollment in Medicaid and lower expected costs per person. CBO now estimates that enrollment in 2022, for example, will be about 84 million, compared with the 85 million it projected last August. Although CBO projects that more people will enroll in Medicaid for the first time because of the Affordable Care Act's expansion of the program, the agency's projection of the number of people who would have been covered by Medicaid in the absence of that act has declined by a greater amount. Lower estimated Medicaid enrollment among those other groups is, in part, the result of improvements in CBO's methods for forecasting the number of people with insurance. More people are now expected to have insurance through other sources (primarily employers), resulting in lower projected enrollment in Medicaid. In addition, fewer people are now expected to enroll in the Supplemental Security Income program, and because people who are enrolled in that program automatically qualify for Medicaid, that change in turn reduces the projected number of Medicaid enrollees. CBO's current baseline also shows lower spending per person in the Medicaid program than was shown in

August, primarily because of adjustments to account for the slowed growth in Medicaid spending. The agency also anticipates that per-person costs will be lower than it anticipated in August because a larger share of the people who will be covered under the Medicaid program will be children and healthier adults, whose medical costs tend to be lower than those of less healthy adults. Because of those and other factors, CBO now estimates that Medicaid's spending per person in 2020 will be about 6 percent lower than it projected in August. (For a discussion, see "Baseline Changes Related to Insurance Coverage Under the Affordable Care Act.")

For Medicare, CBO has reduced its 10-year projections of outlays for Medicare by $137 billion (or 2 percent) for technical reasons, mostly because of updated data on actual spending for 2012, the third consecutive year in which spending was significantly lower than CBO had projected. In past baselines, CBO had begun to reflect the slowing growth in spending for Medicare's Part A (Hospital Insurance) and Part B (Medical Insurance); the largest downward revision in the current baseline is for spending for Medicare's Part D (prescription drugs).[6]

Veterans' Compensation and Pensions

CBO increased its baseline projection for veterans' disability benefits and compensation by $108 billion (or 16 percent) over the 2013–2022 period to reflect substantial recent growth in average benefit payments (the average benefit increased by 8 percent in 2012) and in the number of people added to the disability compensation rolls (there was a 4 percent increase in 2012).

Fannie Mae and Freddie Mac

CBO considers the activities of Fannie Mae and Freddie Mac to be governmental, and therefore it considers the subsidy costs of new activity by the two entities to be federal outlays. The Administration, in contrast, considers the two entities to be outside the federal government for budgetary purposes and records cash transactions between the Treasury and Fannie Mae and Freddie Mac as federal outlays or receipts (in CBO's view, those are intragovernmental transactions).

To provide CBO's best estimate of what the Treasury will ultimately report as the federal deficit for 2013, its current baseline includes an estimate of those net cash transactions for fiscal year 2013. That figure is $29 billion lower than CBO's August estimate, mostly reflecting a shift to a cash-basis estimate for the current year (following the Administration's budgetary treatment for the year in progress) along with an administrative change (agreed to by the Federal Housing Finance Agency and the Treasury Department) that now requires the two entities to convey their quarterly profits to the Treasury rather than paying dividends on outstanding senior preferred stock. CBO's August 2012 baseline showed an estimated subsidy cost (outlays) of about $13 billion for the activities of Fannie Mae and Freddie Mac in 2013; in the current baseline, CBO shows cash receipts—that is, negative outlays—of $17 billion (on the basis of Fannie Mae and Freddie Mac's most recent quarterly financial releases). For 2014 through 2022, CBO's baseline follows the agency's customary approach of showing the projected subsidy costs of credit assistance offered by Fannie Mae and Freddie Mac. Those estimates are calculated on a fair-value basis, reflecting the market risk associated with the two housing entities. For the nine-year period, CBO now estimates that those subsidies will cost the government $35 billion, about $15 billion less than it projected in August. Most of the reduction is the result of an increase in the average fees for new loans and guarantees that Fannie Mae and Freddie Mac implemented at the end of 2012.

Discretionary Spending

Technical adjustments to CBO's projections for several discretionary programs have resulted in a net decrease of $27 billion in outlays estimated for 2013. The largest reductions—which are generally based on slower-than-expected spending— include those in CBO's estimates for the discretionary portion of spending for Pell grants and for certain categories of military spending (mainly operations and maintenance, procurement, and construction).

Changes to projections of discretionary outlays between 2013 and 2022 yield a net decrease of $47 billion (or 0.1 percent), primarily reflecting CBO's expectation that appropriations will be spent at a slightly slower rate, particularly in 2013 and 2014.

Net Interest

As a result of technical updates, CBO's estimates of outlays for net interest have increased by $5 billion for 2013 and by $45 billion for the 2013–2022 period. The increase for the coming decade is mainly attributable to changes in CBO's estimates of the mix of securities that the Treasury will issue, offset partially by a $92 billion reduction in debt service stemming from technical changes in other areas of the budget. To cover the increase in projected deficits relative to those in the August baseline, CBO expects the Treasury to boost borrowing in longer-term and inflation-protected securities, which require higher interest rates than those for nominal securities of shorter maturity. That effect increased projections of interest outlays by about $100 billion for the 2013–2022 period. The remaining $37 billion increase stems from higher expected interest outlays for government securities associated with the Thrift Savings Plan for federal employees and from lower projected interest receipts from the financing accounts associated with the government's credit programs.[7]

Changes to Projections of Revenues

Relative to its August projections, CBO increased its revenue estimates for technical reasons by $63 billion (or 2 percent) for 2013 and by $188 billion (or 2 percent) for the 2014–2016 period. But it has reduced its projections of revenues for the 2017–2022 period by $280 billion (or 1 percent). Over the 2013–2016 period, increases in revenues from individual income taxes and remittances from the Federal Reserve to the Treasury accounted for most of the technical revisions. CBO increased its projection of receipts from individual income taxes by $158 billion relative to its August projection because of larger collections in fiscal year 2012 than the agency had expected in August and because of improvements in CBO's modeling of payments that are made with tax returns. Neither factor affects CBO's forecasts for revenues beyond the next few years. CBO also increased the amount it projects will be made in remittances from the Federal Reserve for the 2013–2016 period. The change reflects larger expected purchases of securities by the central bank, but it also is a result of new modeling that indicates that recent actions by the Federal Reserve to increase the average maturity of its portfolio of Treasury securities will initially result in higher earnings than previously expected. Those remittances are now projected to average about $95 billion per year during that period. Over the 2017–2022 period, decreases in projected revenues from social insurance taxes and remittances from the Federal Reserve account for most of the technical revisions. CBO reduced its estimate of receipts from social insurance taxes throughout the 10-year projection period—and by larger amounts later in the period— mostly because recent tax returns show a smaller amount of wages covered by Social Security than CBO estimated, and the agency expects that pattern to persist in coming years. For the period as a whole, those reductions amounted to about 1 percent of the receipts previously projected from those taxes. CBO reduced its projections of remittances from the Federal Reserve for the second half of the 10-year period, for several reasons. The most significant is that the central bank is now expected to acquire more securities in the short term; the Federal Reserve is expected to shrink the size of its portfolio later in the decade by selling assets, and because interest rates are projected to be higher at that point, those sales will involve capital losses. CBO also now anticipates that the average yield on the Federal Reserve's portfolio will be lower in the second part of the decade because the central bank has locked in today's relatively low interest rates by shifting its portfolio to longer-term securities.

Baseline Changes Related to Insurance Coverage under the Affordable Care Act

In conjunction with JCT, CBO has updated its August 2012 estimate of the budgetary impact of the provisions of the Affordable Care Act that are related to health insurance coverage (see Table A-2).[8] Although several components of the estimate have changed, the difference in the net budgetary impact for the 2013–2022 period is less than $500 million. The new estimate reflects recent legislative, regulatory, and administrative actions along with economic and technical changes made since the previous estimate was published.[9] In August, CBO and JCT projected the net cost of the act's provisions that concern health insurance at $1,165 billion for the 2013–2022 period; that amount remains essentially unchanged. For the 2013–2023 period covered by the current projections (one year beyond the previous ones), the estimated cost of those coverage provisions is $1,329 billion.[10] The most important changes to CBO's estimates include the following:

- Lower marginal tax rates under the American Taxpayer Relief Act reduce the tax benefit associated with employment-based health insurance and will lead to a greater reduction in such coverage and higher enrollment in insurance exchanges than previously estimated by CBO and JCT.
- The Department of Health and Human Services has indicated that, to receive full funding from the federal government for the costs of newly eligible beneficiaries through 2016, states must expand eligibility for Medicaid to the levels specified in the act. Relative to previous projections, that guidance results in a small increase in the estimate of the number of people who will be enrolled in Medicaid and a small reduction in the estimate of the number who will be covered through the exchanges.
- CBO and JCT have slightly reduced their estimates of the rates at which people will enroll in the insurance exchanges or Medicaid as

the expansion of coverage is implemented—a process that had already been anticipated to occur gradually. That change reflects the agencies' judgment about a combination of factors, including the readiness of exchanges to provide a broad array of new insurance options, the ability of state Medicaid programs to absorb new beneficiaries, and people's responses to the availability of the new coverage. As a result, revised estimates for 2014 and 2015 reflect more people with employment-based coverage and more who will be uninsured than in the previous projections. CBO and JCT project that those factors will wane in importance over the following two years. In the current projection, the number of people gaining coverage through the exchanges rises from 7 million in 2014 to 24 million in 2016, and the number gaining coverage through Medicaid rises from 8 million in 2014 to 11 million in 2016.

- CBO and JCT have revised their projections of insurance coverage in the absence of the act. In later years, that revision shows a larger number of people with employment-based coverage and a smaller number without insurance, compared with earlier projections.
- CBO has refined its projections of people's income so that slightly more tax filers and their dependents are now expected to have income that will qualify them for subsidies through the exchanges and for enrollment in Medicaid, resulting in a larger reduction in employment-based coverage in response to changes made by the act than previously had been estimated.
- CBO has revised its analysis of the health status of newly eligible Medicaid enrollees; they now are expected to be healthier and therefore to require less costly care than CBO had previously projected.

Lower Projected Costs for Medicaid and the Children's Health Insurance Program

On net, CBO and JCT project that the Affordable Care Act will increase the number of people enrolled in Medicaid by 12 million in 2022, rather than by the 11 million estimated in August 2012. Despite the difference, the costs for Medicaid and the Children's Health Insurance Program are projected to be $93 billion (or 14 percent) below the earlier projection for the 2013– 2022 period, for several reasons: the revised assessment of the health status of newly eligible enrollees, reductions in the projected cost of Medicaid's benefits generally in response to the recent slowdown in the growth of

Medicaid's spending, and a revised projection that boosts the proportion of children (whose health care generally costs less than that for adults) among the people expected to enroll in Medicaid as a result of the act.

Table A-2. Comparison of CBO's Estimates of the Effects of Insurance Coverage Provisions in the Affordable Care Act

	August 2012 Baseline	February 2013 Baseline	Difference
	Changes in Insurance Coverage in 2022 (Millions of nonelderly people, by calendar year)		
Medicaid and CHIP	11	12	1
Employment-Based[a]	-4	-7	-4
Nongroup and Other[b]	-3	-4	-1
Insurance Exchanges	25	26	*
Uninsured[c]	-30	-27	4
	10-Year Effects on the Federal Deficit, Fiscal Years 2013 to 2022[d,e] (Billions of dollars)		
Medicaid and CHIP Outlays	643	550	-93
Exchange Subsidies and Related Spending[f]	1,015	1,047	32
Small-Employer Tax Creditsg	22	23	1
Gross Cost of Coverage Provisions	1,680	1,620	-60
Penalty Payments by Uninsured Individuals	-55	-45	11
Penalty Payments by Employers[g]	-117	-130	-13
Excise Tax on High-Premium Insurance Plans[g]	-111	-102	9
Other Effects on Tax Revenues and Outlaysh	-231	-178	53
Net Cost of Coverage Provisions	1,165	1,165	**

Sources: Congressional Budget Office; staff of the Joint Committee on Taxation.

Notes: The Affordable Care Act comprises the Patient Protection and Affordable Care Act and the health care provisions of the Health Care and Education Reconciliation Act of 2010 and, in the case of this document, the effects of subsequent related judicial decisions, statutory changes, and administrative actions.

CHIP = Children's Health Insurance Program; * = between zero and 500,000 people; ** = between zero and $500 million.

[a] The change in employment-based coverage is the net result of projected increases in and losses of offers of health insurance from employers and projected changes in enrollment by workers and their families.

[b] The effects are almost entirely for nongroup coverage; "other" includes Medicare.

[c] The count of uninsured people includes unauthorized immigrants as well as people who are eligible for but not enrolled in Medicaid.

[d] Excludes effects on the deficit of other provisions of the act that are not related to coverage, which in the aggregate reduce deficits. Also excludes federal administrative costs subject to appropriation. CBO has previously estimated that the Internal Revenue Service will need to spend between $5 billion and $10 billion over 10 years to implement the Affordable Care Act and that the Department of Health and Human Services and other federal agencies also will have to spend $5 billion to $10 billion over that period. In addition, the Affordable Care Act included explicit authorizations for spending on a variety of grant and other programs; that funding is also subject to future appropriation action.

[e] Negative numbers indicate a decrease in the deficit; positive numbers indicate an increase in the deficit.

[f] Includes spending for high-risk pools, premium review activities, loans to consumer-operated and -oriented plans, and grants to states for the establishment of exchanges.

[g] These effects on the deficit include the associated effects of changes in taxable compensation on revenues.

[h] The effects are almost entirely on revenues.

Higher Enrollment in and Subsidies for Coverage Through Exchanges

CBO and JCT's estimate of the costs of subsidies for insurance obtained through the exchanges and for related spending over the 2013–2022 period is now $32 billion (or about 3 percent) higher than it was in August, mostly because of higher projected enrollment in the exchanges. Lower marginal tax rates under the American Taxpayer Relief Act will reduce the relative attractiveness of employment-based insurance for low-income workers and for their employers. CBO and JCT anticipate that the change in tax law will increase the number of people who shift out of employment-based coverage as a result of the Affordable Care Act by 2 million to 3 million people, many of whom are expected to obtain insurance through the exchanges. Several other technical changes decreased projected enrollment in the exchanges. All told, CBO and JCT now project that 26 million people will be enrolled in the insurance exchanges in 2022, about 500,000 more than estimated in the August 2012 report.

Fewer People with Employment-Based Coverage

In 2022, by CBO and JCT's estimate, 7 million fewer people will have employment-based health insurance as a result of the Affordable Care Act; in August, that figure was estimated to be about 4 million people. The revision is the net effect of several considerations, with the largest factor being the reduction in marginal tax rates, which reduces the tax benefits associated with health insurance provided by employers. The increased movement out of employment-based coverage also reflects revisions to CBO's projections of income over time and higher projections of employment-based coverage in the absence of the Affordable Care Act. Reductions in employment-based health insurance coverage boost federal tax revenues because they increase the proportion of compensation received by workers that is taxable. (That effect is included in Table A-2 in the line labeled "Other Effects on Tax Revenues and Outlays.")

Although a greater reduction in the number of people with employment-based coverage is expected, the projected increase in revenues from changes in the taxability of compensation is now $53 billion less for the 2013– 2022 period than was projected in August because of the lower tax rates enacted in the American Taxpayer Relief Act and because of other technical changes. CBO and JCT have raised their estimate of revenues that will come from penalties paid by employers, by $13 billion for the 2013–2022 period, because fewer businesses are now expected to offer insurance coverage than had been estimated in August.

Penalties arising from the individual mandate are projected to be $11 billion lower than expected in August because, on the basis of revised income projections, more people who remain uninsured are expected either to be exempt from the penalty or to pay a smaller penalty based on a flat rate instead of one based on a percentage of income.

APPENDIX B. CBO'S ECONOMIC PROJECTIONS FOR 2013 TO 2023

The tables in this appendix expand on the information in Section 2 by showing the Congressional Budget Office's (CBO's) economic projections for each year from 2013 to 2023 (by calendar year in Table B-1 and by fiscal year in Table B-2). CBO does not forecast cyclical fluctuations in its projections for years after 2018.

Instead, the projected values shown in the tables for 2019 to 2023 reflect CBO's assessment of the effect of economic and demographic trends in the medium term but do not reflect an attempt to forecast the frequency or size of fluctuations in the business cycle.

Table B-1. CBO's Economic Projections, by Calendar Year

	Estimated, 2012	2013	2014	2015	2016	2017	2018	2019	2020	2021	2022	2023
	Year to Year (Percentage change)											
Real GDP	2.3	1.4	2.6	4.1	4.4	3.8	2.6	2.4	2.3	2.2	2.2	2.2
Nominal GDP	4.1	2.9	4.4	6.2	6.6	6.0	4.7	4.5	4.4	4.3	4.3	4.2
PCE Price Index	1.7	1.3	1.7	1.9	1.9	1.9	2.0	2.0	2.0	2.0	2.0	2.0
Core PCE Price Index[a]	1.7	1.3	1.8	1.9	1.9	2.0	2.0	2.0	2.0	2.0	2.0	2.0
Consumer Price Index[b]	2.1 c	1.6	1.9	2.1	2.1	2.2	2.3	2.3	2.3	2.3	2.3	2.3
Core Consumer Price Index[a]	2.1 c	1.7	2.0	2.1	2.2	2.3	2.3	2.3	2.3	2.3	2.3	2.3
GDP Price Index	1.8	1.5	1.8	2.0	2.1	2.1	2.1	2.0	2.1	2.0	2.0	2.0
Employment Cost Index[d]	1.8	2.1	2.9	3.9	4.0	4.2	4.0	3.8	3.7	3.6	3.6	3.5
					Calendar Year Average							
Unemployment Rate (Percent)	8.1 c	7.9	7.8	7.1	6.3	5.6	5.5	5.5	5.4	5.4	5.3	5.3
Payroll Employment												
(Monthly change, in thousands)	157 c	105	182	222	220	153	88	86	82	80	66	62
Interest Rates (Percent)												
Three-month Treasury bills	0.1 c	0.1	0.2	0.2	1.5	3.4	4.0	4.0	4.0	4.0	4.0	4.0
Ten-year Treasury notes	1.8 c	2.1	2.7	3.5	4.3	5.0	5.2	5.2	5.2	5.2	5.2	5.2
Tax Bases (Percentage of GDP)												
Wages and salaries	44.1	43.5	43.9	44.0	44.1	44.2	44.5	44.6	44.8	44.9	45.1	45.2
Domestic economic profits	9.6	9.3	9.7	9.9	10.2	9.8	9.0	8.4	8.0	7.7	7.5	7.2

	Estimated, 2012	2013	2014	2015	2016	2017	2018	2019	2020	2021	2022	2023
Tax Bases (Billions of dollars)												
Wages and salaries	6,916	7,029	7,397	7,876	8,410	8,946	9,414	9,872	10,343	10,827	11,326	11,835
Domestic economic profits	1,509	1,506	1,629	1,782	1,944	1,973	1,913	1,863	1,847	1,858	1,876	1,893
Nominal GDP (Billions of dollars)	15,692	16,149	16,863	17,913	19,087	20,224	21,178	22,129	23,099	24,093	25,117	26,180

Source: Congressional Budget Office. (Actual values for 2012 are from Department of Labor, Bureau of Labor Statistics; Federal Reserve.)

Notes: The numbers shown here do not reflect the values for GDP and related series released by the Commerce Department's Bureau of Economic Analysis on January 30 and the values released by the Labor Department's Bureau of Labor Statistics for the employment cost index on January 31 and for payroll employment on February 1.

GDP = gross domestic product; PCE = personal consumption expenditures.

a Excludes prices for food and energy.

b The consumer price index for all urban consumers.

c Actual value for 2012.

d The employment cost index for wages and salaries of workers in private industry.

Table B-2. CBO's Economic Projections, by Fiscal Year

	Actual, 2012	2013	2014	2015	2016	2017	2018	2019	2020	2021	2022	2023
				Year to Year (Percentage change)								
Real GDP	2.3	1.5	2.1	3.9	4.4	4.0	2.8	2.4	2.3	2.2	2.2	2.2
Nominal GDP	4.2	3.1	3.8	5.9	6.6	6.2	4.9	4.5	4.4	4.3	4.3	4.2
PCE Price Index	2.0	1.3	1.5	1.9	1.9	1.9	2.0	2.0	2.0	2.0	2.0	2.0
Core PCE Price Index[a]	1.8	1.3	1.7	1.9	1.9	2.0	2.0	2.0	2.0	2.0	2.0	2.0

Table B-2. (Continued)

	Actual, 2012	2013	2014	2015	2016	2017	2018	2019	2020	2021	2022	2023
Consumer Price Index[b]	2.4	1.7	1.7	2.1	2.1	2.2	2.3	2.3	2.3	2.3	2.3	2.3
Core Consumer Price Index[a]	2.2	1.7	1.9	2.1	2.1	2.2	2.3	2.3	2.3	2.3	2.3	2.3
GDP Price Index	1.8	1.5	1.7	2.0	2.1	2.1	2.1	2.1	2.0	2.1	2.0	2.0
Employment Cost Index[c]	1.8	2.0	2.6	3.7	4.0	4.1	4.1	3.9	3.7	3.6	3.6	3.6
					Fiscal Year Average							
Unemployment Rate (Percent)	8.3	7.9	7.9	7.3	6.5	5.7	5.5	5.5	5.4	5.4	5.3	5.3
Payroll Employment												
(Monthly change, in thousands)	157	110	156	224	223	183	91	84	84	80	70	63
Interest Rates (Percent)												
Three-month Treasury bills	0.1	0.1	0.1	0.2	1.0	2.9	4.0	4.0	4.0	4.0	4.0	4.0
Ten-year Treasury notes	1.9	1.9	2.5	3.2	4.1	4.9	5.2	5.2	5.2	5.2	5.2	5.2
Tax Bases (Percentage of GDP)												
Wages and salaries	43.8	43.7	43.9	43.9	44.0	44.2	44.4	44.6	44.7	44.9	45.1	45.2
Domestic economic profits	9.7	9.4	9.5	9.9	10.2	9.9	9.2	8.6	8.1	7.8	7.5	7.3
Tax Bases (Billions of dollars)												
Wages and salaries	6,812	7,014	7,300	7,748	8,274	8,818	9,300	9,757	10,224	10,704	11,201	11,707
Domestic economic profits	1,506	1,503	1,589	1,742	1,913	1,978	1,929	1,873	1,847	1,854	1,871	1,890
Nominal GDP (Billions of dollars)	15,549	16,034	16,646	17,632	18,792	19,959	20,943	21,890	22,854	23,842	24,858	25,910

Source: Congressional Budget Office. (Actual values for 2012 are from Department of Commerce, Bureau of Economic Analysis; Department of Labor, Bureau of Labor Statistics; Federal Reserve.)

Note: GDP = gross domestic product; PCE = personal consumption expenditures.

[a] Excludes prices for food and energy.

[b] The consumer price index for all urban consumers.

[c] The employment cost index for wages and salaries of workers in private industry.

End Notes for Section 1

[1] For a discussion of the consequences of elevated debt, see Congressional Budget Office, *Choices for Deficit Reduction* (November 2012), p.10, www.cbo.gov/publication/43692.

[2] For a more detailed discussion of the long-term budget situation, see Congressional Budget Office, *The 2012 Long-Term Budget Outlook* (June 2012), www.cbo.gov/publication /43288. CBO has not yet updated its long-term projections to reflect the effects of the American Taxpayer Relief Act (P.L. 112-240) or other changes to its 10-year projections that have occurred since June 2012.

[3] For CBO's previous baseline budget projections, see Congressional Budget Office, *An Update to the Budget and Economic Outlook: Fiscal Years 2012 to 2022* (August 2012), www.cbo.gov/publication/43539.

[4] The size of those automatic reductions will be determined by the Office of Management and Budget, which has not yet indicated what they will be. Most large nondefense programs (including, for example, Social Security, Medicaid, unemployment compensation, and veterans' benefits) are exempted from those cuts, and the reduction in Medicare is limited to 2 percent.

[5] According to the rules for sequestration, reductions in Medicare will begin in the month after the sequestration order is issued, thereby delaying some of the effect on outlays until the following fiscal year. In addition, discretionary funding in subsequent years will be cut by roughly $90 billion annually as a result of the automatic reductions.

[6] The shifting of income will reduce revenues over time by moving the income into a year with lower tax rates. CBO estimates that the most significant shifting of revenues between those two years occurred for capital gains realizations; the revenue effects from shifts in wages and salaries occur largely within fiscal year 2013.

[7] Present value is a single number that expresses a flow of current and future income (or payments) in terms of an equivalent lump sum received (or paid) today.

[8] CBO now estimates that the TARP will cost $22 billion (excluding administrative costs) over its lifetime.

[9] Emergency unemployment benefits are currently available through December 2013. The maximum number of weeks that the long-term unemployed can receive benefits depends on the unemployment rate of the state in which they worked. Under current law, a state must have an unemployment rate at or above 9 percent in order to provide benefits for the maximum number of weeks under that program. The payment of extended benefits also requires a state's unemployment rate to be relatively high. For example, in order to provide extended benefits, a state's unemployment rate must not only exceed a certain threshold but it must be rising relative to recent unemployment rates in that state.

[10] For fiscal year 2013, the security category comprises discretionary appropriations for the Departments of Defense, Homeland Security, and Veterans Affairs; the National Nuclear Security Administration; the intelligence community management account (Treasury account 95-0401-0-1-054); and discretionary accounts related to international affairs (budget function 150). The nonsecurity category comprises all other discretionary appropriations.

[11] Roughly three-quarters of that amount is a longer-term effect that results from increases in the potential output of the economy (that is, the maximum sustainable level of economic output), and the rest results from the return of output to its potential level over the next several years.

[12] The Affordable Care Act comprises the Patient Protection and Affordable Care Act (P.L. 111-148) and the health care provisions of the Health Care and Education Reconciliation Act of 2010 (P.L. 111-152) and, in the case of this document, the effects of subsequent related judicial decisions, statutory changes, and administrative actions.

[13] The Federal Reserve's remittances would not drop below zero. Rather, the net losses that CBO projects for 2018 and 2019 would be carried forward and netted against future payments.

[14] The federal funds rate is the interest rate that financial institutions charge each other for overnight loans of their monetary reserves.

[15] The Deficit Control Act specifies some exceptions. For example, spending programs whose authorizations are set to expire are assumed to continue if they have outlays of more than $50 million in the current year and were established at or before the enactment of the Balanced Budget Act of 1997. Programs established after that law was enacted are not automatically assumed to continue but are considered individually in consultation with the budget committees.

[16] Under CBO's baseline, outlays are projected to remain steady at 22.9 percent of GDP in 2022 and 2023. That result is largely attributable to a shift in the timing of certain payments. Because both October 1, 2022, and October 1, 2023, fall on weekends, certain payments that are due on those days will instead be made at the end of September, thus shifting them into the previous fiscal year. Without that shift, under CBO's baseline, outlays would increase from 22.7 percent of GDP in 2022 to 22.9 percent in 2023.

[17] Subsidies for assistance with premiums will be given in the form of refundable tax credits, which are recorded as budget outlays to the extent that they exceed taxpayers' other liabilities and as reductions in revenues to the extent that they reduce people's tax payments. Some individuals and families will qualify for additional subsidies to reduce their out-of-pocket costs; those subsidies are classified entirely as outlays.

[18] The caps also may be adjusted upward to allow additional spending for program integrity initiatives, which identify and reduce overpayments in certain benefit programs, as well as for some funding for emergencies and disaster relief.

[19] A small amount of debt held by the public is issued by other agencies, mainly the Tennessee Valley Authority.

[20] That act also contained $5 billion in funding designated as disaster funding (as defined in the Budget Control Act) and $3 billion that was not designated as emergency funding; both types of funding are extrapolated in CBO's baseline but are subject to constraints in future years.

[21] The estimated cost of holding payment rates constant is much lower relative to this baseline than was the case under previous CBO baselines, primarily because of lower spending for physicians' services in recent years. Under the sustainable growth rate, future payment updates depend on the difference between spending in prior years and spending targets established in law. Actual spending has been lower than projected—and lower than the spending targets inherent in the sustainable growth rate—for the past three years. Because actual spending has been lower than spending targets, CBO now estimates that payment rates will increase beginning in 2015. Those higher payment rates narrow the difference between growth under current law and a freeze at current levels, thereby reducing the estimated cost of restricting the payment rates.

[22] Budgetary resources subject to sequestration include new budget authority, unobligated balances for defense programs, and direct spending authority.

[23] Because of interactions between the effects of different policy options, the estimated budgetary effects of this option cannot be added to the estimated budgetary effects of any of the

alternatives that affect discretionary spending other than the one to reduce the number of troops deployed for overseas contingency operations.

End Notes for Section 2

1 An alternative fiscal scenario that incorporates one particular set of policies implying less fiscal tightening is detailed in Section 1. CBO has not quantified the economic effects of that scenario.

2 For a discussion of the fiscal tightening that was scheduled to occur in 2013, see Congressional Budget Office, *Economic Effects of Policies Contributing to Fiscal Tightening in 2013* (November 2012), www.cbo.gov/publication/43694.

3 For a discussion of the economic expansion since the end of the recession, see Congressional Budget Office, *What Accounts for the Slow Growth of the Economy After the Recession?* (November 2012), www.cbo.gov/publication/43707.

4 This report was prepared before the release of data for the fourth quarter of 2012 by the Commerce Department's Bureau of Economic Analysis on January 30. According to that release, GDP grew more slowly in 2012 than CBO had estimated (1.5 percent instead of 1.9 percent) because GDP growth in the fourth quarter was well below CBO's estimate. However, growth in the fourth quarter was held down by several temporary developments, including large drops in defense spending and inventory investment, that are not expected to recur. Apart from those two developments, which reduced GDP growth in the fourth quarter by 2.6 percentage points, underlying momentum in the economy appears moderately strong, with gains in consumer spending, noninventory investment by businesses, and residential construction. Consequently, incorporating the fourth quarter data would have had only a small effect on CBO's projections.

5 For additional discussion, see Ben S. Bernanke, "Recent Developments in the Labor Market" (address given at the National Association for Business Economics Annual Conference, Arlington, Va., March 26, 2012), www.federalreserve.gov/newsevents/ speech/bernanke 20120326a.htm.

6 For further discussion of structural unemployment and the weak labor market of the past few years, see Congressional Budget Office, *Understanding and Responding to Persistently High Unemployment* (February 2012), www.cbo.gov/publication/42989.

7 According to the January 30 release of fourth quarter data by the Bureau of Economic Analysis, the PCE price index and the core PCE price index grew by 1.5 percent last year.

8 For discussions of the Federal Reserve's nontraditional policy actions of the past few years and their effects on the economy, see Arvind Krishnamurthy and Annette Vissing-Jorgensen, *The Effects of Quantitative Easing on Interest Rates: Channels and Implications for Policy,* Working Paper 17555 (National Bureau of Economic Research, October 2011), www.nber.org/papers/w17555; and Brett W. Fawley and Christopher J. Neely, "Four Stories of Quantitative Easing," *Review*, Federal Reserve Bank of St. Louis, vol. 95, no. 1 (January/February 2013), pp. 51–88, http://research.stlouisfed.org/publications /review /13/01/ Fawley.pdf.

9 That estimate is informed by recent changes to law and CBO's previous analysis of the effects on GDP of fiscal tightening in 2013. See Congressional Budget Office, *Economic Effects of Policies Contributing to Fiscal Tightening in 2013* (November 2012), www.cbo.gov /publication/43694.

[10] For discussions of unusual features of the current business cycle, see, for example, Congressional Budget Office, *The Budget and Economic Outlook: Fiscal Years 2011 to 2021* (January 2011), pp. 28–36, www.cbo.gov/publication/21999, and *What Accounts for the Slow Growth of the Economy After the Recession?* (November 2012), www.cbo.gov/publication/43707.

[11] With that pace of growth in the labor force and a steady unemployment rate, CBO projects that payroll employment will increase by 75,000 per month during the 2019–2023 period, also well below its historical average.

[12] For more discussion of those effects, see Congressional Budget Office, *An Update to the Budget and Economic Outlook: Fiscal Years 2012 to 2022* (August 2012), Box 2-2, www.cbo.gov/publication/ 43539.

[13] CBO defines labor income as the sum of employees' compensation and a percentage of proprietors' income, where that percentage equals employees' compensation as a share of the difference between GDI and proprietors' income. In the past, CBO defined labor income as the sum of employees' compensation and 65 percent of proprietors' income, following the convention used most often in the economics literature. However, CBO recently reassessed its allocation of proprietors' income among the categories of labor and capital income in light of new research. See Congressional Budget Office, *The Taxation of Capital and Labor Through the Self-Employment Tax* (September 2012), pp. 16–17, www.cbo.gov/publication/43644.

[14] Domestic economic profits are corporations' domestic profits adjusted to remove distortions in depreciation allowances caused by tax rules and to exclude the effects of inflation on the value of inventories. Domestic economic profits exclude certain income of U.S.-based multinational corporations that is derived from foreign sources, most of which does not generate corporate income tax receipts in the United States.

End Notes for Appendix A

[1] Those projections were reported in Congressional Budget Office, *An Update to the Budget and Economic Outlook: Fiscal Years 2012 to 2022* (August 2012), www.cbo.gov /publication/43539.

CBO constructs its baseline in accordance with provisions of the Balanced Budget and Emergency Deficit Control Act of 1985 and the Congressional Budget and Impoundment Control Act of 1974. To project revenues and mandatory spending, CBO assumes that current laws, with only a few exceptions, will remain unchanged. To project discretionary spending, CBO assumes that appropriations through 2021 will adhere to the caps and automatic spending reductions referenced in the Budget Control Act of 2011 (Public Law 112-25) and that appropriations for 2022 and 2023 will grow from the 2021 amount at the rate of inflation. The resulting baseline projections are not intended to be a prediction of future budgetary outcomes; rather, they serve as a benchmark that lawmakers can use to measure the potential effects of tax or spending proposals.

[2] The Affordable Care Act comprises the Patient Protection and Affordable Care Act (P.L. 111-148) and the health care provisions of the Health Care and Education Reconciliation Act of 2010 (P.L. 111-152) and, in the case of this document, the effects of subsequent related judicial decisions, statutory changes, and administrative actions.

[3] Overall, CBO estimates that the American Taxpayer Relief Act will increase Medicare's outlays by $5 billion for the 2013–2022 period; taking account of the effects of provisions of the legislation related to other health care programs yields a net increase for the period of about $1 billion in outlays for such programs (including Medicare).

[4] A basis point is one one-hundredth of a percentage point. For example, the difference between interest rates of 1.0 percent and 1.5 percent is 50 basis points.

[5] Present value is a single number that expresses a flow of current and future income (or payments) in terms of an equivalent lump sum received (or paid) today.

[6] Since 2009, spending for Part A and Part B has risen by an average of 2.9 percent per year, compared with average annual growth of 8.4 percent from 2002 to 2009. (That comparison excludes spending for Part D because the growth rates for fiscal years 2006 and 2007 were affected by the program's establishment in 2006.)

[7] The Thrift Savings Plan is a retirement savings program for civil service employees and members of the uniformed services. Like private-sector 401(k) plans, the Thrift Savings Plan offers federal employees an opportunity to invest in funds that hold different sorts of financial assets, including domestic and foreign stocks, and U.S. government securities, which are nonmarketable Treasury securities issued specifically for the program. Those securities have short maturities but earn a long-term interest rate equal to the weighted average market yield on outstanding marketable Treasury securities with four or more years to maturity.

[8] Details of the current estimate are posted along with this report on CBO's Web site, www.cbo.gov/publication/43900.

[9] The current budget baseline does not incorporate the effects of regulations and guidance issued in late December 2012 and January 2013 by the Department of the Treasury and the Department of Health and Human Services.

[10] Those sums, which include effects on both revenues and outlays, do not reflect the total budgetary impact of the legislation. The law included many other provisions that, on net, will reduce budget deficits; on balance, CBO and JCT have estimated that the legislation as a whole will reduce deficits over a 10-year period. CBO and JCT have not updated their estimates of the total budgetary impact of the Affordable Care Act. For CBO and JCT's most recent estimate of the budgetary impact of repealing the act, see Congressional Budget Office, letter to the Honorable John Boehner providing an estimate for H.R. 6079, the Repeal of Obamacare Act (July 24, 2012), www.cbo.gov/publication/ 43471.

In: Budgetary and Economic Outlooks to 2023 ... ISBN: 978-1-62618-760-3
Editor: Liam Krause © 2013 Nova Science Publishers, Inc.

Chapter 2

MACROECONOMIC EFFECTS OF ALTERNATIVE BUDGETARY PATHS*

Benjamin Page

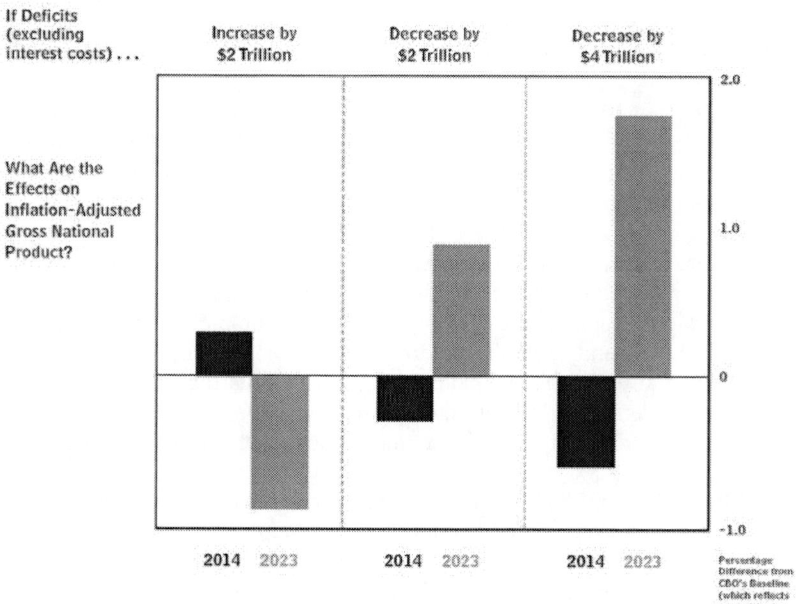

* Benjamin Page wrote this report which was released by the Congressional Budget Office, dated February 2013.

NOTE

Numbers in the text and tables may not add up to totals because of rounding.

SUMMARY

Federal debt held by the public now exceeds 70 percent of the nation's annual output (gross domestic product, or GDP) and stands at a higher percentage than in any year since 1950. Under an assumption whereby current laws generally remain unchanged, federal debt will be 77 percent of GDP in 2023, the Congressional Budget Office (CBO) projects.[1] Such a large amount of federal debt will reduce the nation's output and income below what would occur if the debt was smaller, and it raises the risk of a fiscal crisis (in which the government would lose the ability to borrow money at affordable interest rates). Moreover, the aging of the population and rising health care costs will tend to push debt even higher in the following decades.

In addition, those projections of debt under current law incorporate scheduled changes in policies that will serve to restrain the growth of debt. For example, under current law, some significant tax provisions will expire at the end of this year or in later years, increasing revenues; automatic spending cuts included in the Budget Control Act of 2011 and modified in the American Taxpayer Relief Act of 2012 will go into effect on March 1, 2013; and Medicare's payment rates for physicians' services will fall in January 2014. If future legislation prevented those changes from taking effect and did not make other policy changes with offsetting budgetary effects, federal debt would be considerably higher than the amount projected under current law.

To aid lawmakers in assessing the macroeconomic effects of possible changes in tax and spending policies, this report describes the effects of three alternative budgetary paths: one with deficits that are greater than those projected under current law and two with deficits that are smaller. Those paths are purely illustrative and do not represent recommendations by CBO.

In evaluating policy changes that would change projected budget deficits, lawmakers would undoubtedly weigh other considerations besides the macroeconomic effects—taking into account, for example, views about the proper size of the federal government and the best allocation of its resources. Lawmakers would also be concerned about the distributional implications of proposed changes—that is, who would bear the burden of any cuts in spending or increases in taxes (or who would benefit from spending increases or tax cuts), and who would gain or lose from changes in economic conditions. Such considerations are outside the scope of this analysis but have been addressed by CBO in other reports.[2]

What Budgetary Paths Did CBO Analyze?

CBO analyzed three budgetary paths that would alter cumulative primary deficits (that is, deficits excluding interest costs) from 2014 to 2023 relative to those under current law—an increase of $2 trillion (Path 1), a decrease of $2 trillion (Path 2), and a decrease of $4 trillion (Path 3). In each case, the budgetary changes would begin in 2014 and increase steadily over time.

The changes in primary deficits that occurred under the three paths would induce changes in debt service (the interest the government pays on its debt). They would also affect the economy, which would have further budgetary consequences (mostly through the rate of economic growth and interest rates). As a result, CBO estimates, the changes in total deficits and in federal debt held by the public from 2014 through 2023 would be as follows:

- *Path 1: A $2 Trillion Increase in Primary Deficits.* With economic effects and debt service included, the cumulative increase in the deficit would total $2.5 trillion and debt would reach 87 percent of GDP in 2023, compared with, respectively, 73 percent at the end of 2012 and 77 percent projected for fiscal year 2023 under current law (see Figure 1).
- *Path 2: A $2 Trillion Reduction in Primary Deficits.* The total cumulative decrease in the deficit would amount to $2.4 trillion and debt would drop to 67 percent of GDP in fiscal year 2023.[3]
- *Path 3: A $4 Trillion Reduction in Primary Deficits.* The total cumulative decrease in the deficit would amount to $4.8 trillion and debt would drop to 58 percent of GDP in fiscal year 2023.

For the sake of simplicity and to avoid any presumption about what particular policies might be chosen to reduce the deficit, CBO has not specified fiscal policies underlying the three illustrative paths. As a result, the projected outcomes under the three paths reflect no direct changes to the incentives to work and save that exist under current law; for example, marginal tax rates (the rates that apply to an additional dollar of a taxpayer's income) are assumed to be the same as those under current law. Therefore, the estimated macroeconomic effects presented in this report arise solely from the differences in deficits, and not from any effects of different tax policies or benefit programs that would directly alter people's incentives to work and save.

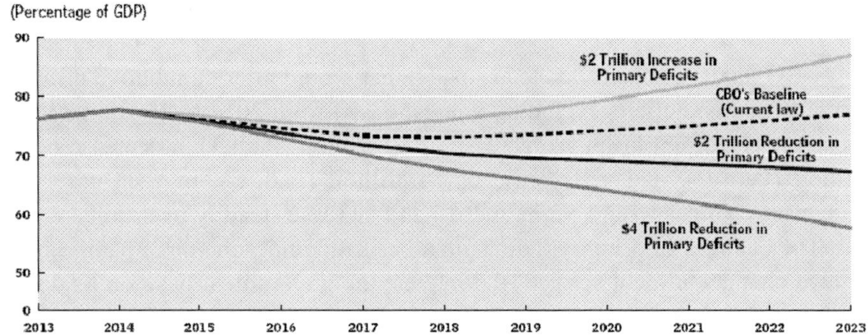

Source: Congressional Budget Office.

Notes: The illustrative paths are described in detail in the text, at the beginning of the section titled "Budget Deficits Under Three Illustrative Paths."

The primary deficit equals revenues minus noninterest spending.

GDP = gross domestic product.

Figure 1. Debt Held by the Public Under Current Law and the Illustrative Paths, Including Economic Effects, Fiscal Years 2013 to 2023.

In fact, changing budget deficits significantly relative to what would occur under current law without altering incentives to work and save would be very difficult. If policies that raised or lowered deficits affected those incentives, then the overall economic impact of those policies would depend on both the changes in federal borrowing and the changes in incentives. In addition, the short-run economic impact of deficits would differ depending on how the specific tax and spending policies affected aggregate demand.[4]

How Would Such Budgetary Paths Affect the Economy?

In assessing the effects of the budgetary paths on total economic output, CBO focused on changes in gross national product (GNP). Unlike the more commonly cited GDP, GNP excludes foreigners' earnings on investments in the domestic economy but includes U.S. residents' earnings overseas; changes in GNP are therefore a better measure of the effects of policies on U.S. residents' income than are changes in GDP.

Relative to projections under current law, CBO estimates, policies that led to larger deficits by raising spending or cutting taxes would boost GNP from 2014 to 2016, and policies that reduced deficits by cutting spending or raising taxes would lower GNP in those years—reflecting the short-term impact of tax and spending policies on the demand for goods and services. By contrast, sustained higher deficits would lead to lower GNP beginning in 2017, and sustained lower deficits would lead to higher GNP beginning then—reflecting the impact of deficits on national saving and domestic investment (and without accounting for any changes to households' incentives to work or save stemming from changes to tax policies or benefit programs).

Compared with the agency's baseline projections (reflecting current law), the illustrative paths would have differing effects on GNP at the end of next year and after a decade:

- *Path 1: A $2 Trillion Increase in Primary Deficits.* Real (inflation-adjusted) GNP would be higher, by 0.3 percent, in the fourth quarter of 2014 and lower, by 0.9 percent, in 2023 than it would be under current law (see Table 1).
- *Path 2: A $2 Trillion Reduction in Primary Deficits.* Real GNP would be lower, by 0.3 percent, in the fourth quarter of 2014 and higher, by 0.9 percent, in 2023 than it would be under current law.
- *Path 3: A $4 trillion Reduction in Primary Deficits.* Real GNP would be lower, by 0.6 percent, in the fourth quarter of 2014 and higher, by 1.7 percent, in 2023 than it would be under current law.

Those findings represent CBO's central estimates, but to reflect the high degree of uncertainty involved, the agency also estimated a range of effects encompassing a broad span of economists' views about the relevant economic relationships.

Of course, policy changes of many other sizes and different patterns over time are possible, as are combinations of policies. For example, if policymakers wanted to raise GNP in the near term relative to projections under current law, as well as raise GNP in later years relative to that same benchmark, they could enact a combination of policies that increased deficits during the next few years and decreased them by a greater cumulative amount thereafter (ultimately leading to less debt than would arise under current law). That approach, however, would allow more federal debt to accumulate over the next few years and might raise doubts about whether long-term deficit reduction would actually take place. Households, businesses, state and local governments, and participants in the financial markets would be more likely to believe that the deficit reduction would truly take effect in the future if the future policy changes were specific and widely supported.

BUDGET DEFICITS UNDER THREE ILLUSTRATIVE PATHS

The three paths analyzed by CBO vary in the magnitude and direction of their budgetary changes but are phased in with the same timing. The impact of the paths is shown in terms of both the *primary budget deficit*, which is the difference between revenues and noninterest spending (excluding the costs of servicing the government's debt), and the *total deficit*, which is the difference between revenues and all spending. In addition, total deficits are shown both excluding and including the macroeconomic impact of the changes in budget deficits. The effect of a policy change on the primary deficit excluding the macroeconomic effects is the number that would be provided in a standard CBO cost estimate for a legislative proposal. The effect of a policy change on the total deficit including the overall economic impact corresponds to the change in the deficit that would be included in CBO's baseline projections once that policy change was incorporated into the baseline. (Of course, an updated baseline would also include the effects of other legislative actions, other changes in the economic projections, and changes in the agency's technical assumptions.)

Path 1: A $2 Trillion Increase in Primary Deficits

Cumulatively over fiscal years 2014 to 2023, deficits under Path 1 would exceed those under current law by $2.3 trillion—consisting of a $2.0 trillion increase in primary deficits and a $0.3 trillion increase in interest costs (see Table 2). The increases in primary deficits would begin at $40 billion in fiscal year 2014 and rise steadily, reaching $360 billion in fiscal year 2023. (Those budgetary changes, as well as those in the descriptions of Paths 2 and 3 below, do not include the budgetary impact of the economic effects of the paths, which are discussed in later sections of the report.)

Table 1. Effects of Illustrative Paths on Real GNP in Selected Calendar Years, Relative to Projections Under Current Law (Percentage difference)

	Short Term (2014)	Longer Term (2023)
$2 Trillion Increase in Primary Deficits		
Central estimate	0.3	-0.9
Range	0.1 to 0.5	-1.3 to -0.5
$2 Trillion Reduction in Primary Deficits		
Central estimate	-0.3	0.9
Range	-0.5 to -0.1	0.5 to 1.3
$4 Trillion Reduction in Primary Deficits		
Central estimate	-0.6	1.7
Range	-1.0 to -0.2	0.9 to 2.5

Source: Congressional Budget Office.

Notes: The illustrative paths are described in detail in the text, at the beginning of the section titled "Budget Deficits Under Three Illustrative Paths."

The primary deficit equals revenues minus noninterest spending.

Figures reflect the percentage difference (in the fourth quarter levels) between a path's effects and the outcomes under CBO's baseline, which incorporates the assumption that current laws generally remain unchanged.

Ranges of estimated effects are shown to reflect the uncertainty that exists about many of the economic relationships that are important in the models used to calculate those effects.

Real GNP = inflation-adjusted gross national product.

Path 2: A $2 Trillion Reduction in Primary Deficits

Path 2 is a mirror image of Path 1: Cumulatively, over fiscal years 2014 to 2023, deficits under Path 2 would fall below those under current law by $2.3 trillion—consisting of a $2.0 trillion decrease in primary deficits and a $0.3 billion decrease in interest costs. The decreases in primary deficits would begin at $40 billion in fiscal year 2014 and rise steadily, reaching $360 billion in fiscal year 2023.

Table 2. Effects of Illustrative Paths on the Budget Without Economic Effects, Relative to Projections under Current Law, Fiscal Years 2014 to 2023 (Billions of dollars)

	2014	2015	2016	2017	2018	2019	2020	2021	2022	2023	2014-2023
	Increases (-) in Deficits										
$2 Trillion Increase in Primary Deficits Effect on primary deficits	-40	-76	-111	-147	-182	-218	-253	-289	-324	-360	-2,000
Debt service	0	-1	-4	-10	-20	-29	-41	-55	-72	-91	-322
Effect on total deficits	-40	-76	-115	-156	-202	-247	-294	-344	-396	-451	-2,322
	Decreases (+) in Deficits										
$2 Trillion Reduction in Primary Deficits											
Effect on primary deficits	40	76	111	147	182	218	253	289	324	360	2,000
Debt service	0	1	4	10	20	29	41	55	72	91	322
Effect on total deficits	40	76	115	156	202	247	294	344	396	451	2,322
$4 Trillion Reduction in Primary Deficits											
Effect on primary deficits	80	151	222	293	364	436	507	578	649	720	4,000
Debt service	1	1	8	19	39	58	81	111	144	182	643
Effect on total deficits	81	152	230	312	404	493	588	688	793	902	4,643
Memorandum:											
CBO's February 2013 Baseline											
Primary deficit (-) or surplus	-373	-158	-153	-123	-88	-117	-131	-123	-163	-120	-1,549
Net interest (-)	-243	-272	-323	-412	-517	-593	-667	-730	-795	-857	-5,410
Total deficit	-616	-430	-476	-535	-605	-710	-798	-854	-957	-978	-6,958

Source: Congressional Budget Office.

Notes: The illustrative paths are described in detail in the text, at the beginning of the section titled "Budget Deficits Under Three Illustrative Paths."

The primary deficit equals revenues minus noninterest spending. Debt service is the change in the deficit that would result from changes in the amount of interest paid on the public debt.

The effect on total deficits is the sum of the effect on primary deficits and debt service.

Negative numbers indicate that deficits under the path are larger than those under CBO's baseline, which incorporates the assumption that current laws generally remain unchanged; positive amounts indicate that deficits are smaller.

Path 3: A $4 Trillion Reduction in Primary Deficits

Path 3 doubles the budgetary changes of Path 2. Cumulatively, over fiscal years 2014 to 2023, deficits under Path 3 would fall below those under current law by $4.6 trillion—consisting of a $4.0 trillion decrease in primary deficits and a $0.6 billion decrease in interest costs. The decreases in primary deficits would begin at $80 billion in fiscal year 2014 and rise steadily, reaching $720 billion in fiscal year 2023.

CBO's Analytical Approach

CBO used two approaches to estimate the economic effects of the three illustrative paths relative to the agency's February 2013 baseline economic forecast, which incorporates the assumption that current laws generally remain unchanged. Those approaches focus on somewhat different aspects of the economy and reflect distinct ways of thinking about it. One approach addresses short-term effects that stem largely from variations in aggregate demand; the other addresses medium-term and long-term effects on the economy's potential output. Each approach represents people's economic decisions in a simplified way while capturing some important aspects of their behavior. (For additional details on the approaches, see Appendix A.)

The three paths do not incorporate any assumptions about the particular mix of spending or revenue changes used to accomplish increases or reductions in deficits and are not meant to correspond to any specific legislative proposals. Therefore, CBO assumed that each path would have the same marginal tax rates as those under current law. Because the unspecified policies that differentiate the paths were assumed to have no direct effect on the incentives to work and save, they differ in their economic effects only because of differences in the magnitude of budget deficits; those differences affect the economy primarily by altering the demand for goods and services in the next few years and national saving and investment later in the decade and beyond.

In estimating the short-run economic effects of those unspecified policies for deficit reduction, CBO assumed for its central estimates that each $1 change in primary budget deficits relative to those under current law would change output cumulatively by $1 over several quarters. That dollar-for-dollar response lies within the ranges of estimated effects on GDP of many policies examined in CBO's analysis of the macroeconomic effects of the American

Recovery and Reinvestment Act of 2009 (ARRA). For its full range of estimates, CBO assumed that each $1 change in primary deficits would change output cumulatively by between $0.33 and $1.67. That range of possible effects on output, reflecting the uncertainty surrounding the possible outcomes, is about the same (in percentage terms) as the range between low and high estimates of the effects on output of particular policies in the analysis of ARRA.[5]

In this analysis, CBO reports effects of fiscal policy on GNP and the interest rate on 10-year Treasury notes. Changes in GNP are a better measure of the effects on U.S. residents' income than are changes in GDP—the more common measure of the economy's output. Because larger budget deficits generate larger inflows of capital from other countries, they imply that a growing portion of the nation's income would have to be sent abroad as returns (in the form of profits or interest) on that invested capital and thus would not be available to U.S. households. GNP would reflect such developments.

CBO did not estimate the effects of the paths on employment and unemployment. In general, if changes in budget deficits raise output in the short term, they will also raise employment and lower the unemployment rate. In the longer term, the economy is assumed to be operating near or at its maximum sustainable level, so changes in output caused by changes in budget deficits will be reflected primarily in productivity and wages rather than employment and unemployment (although changes in after-tax wages would have some effect on participation in the labor force and employment).

As in previous analyses of this sort, CBO has estimated the budgetary implications of the illustrative paths' macroeconomic effects using a simplified approach that takes into account the effects of changes in GNP, interest rates, and other factors.[6] Those effects include the following, for example: Higher output implies higher taxable incomes and, therefore, increased tax revenues; and higher interest rates imply greater interest payments on the public debt and, therefore, more spending.

MACROECONOMIC EFFECTS OF CHANGES IN BUDGET DEFICITS

According to CBO's baseline economic projections, real GNP under current law will grow by 1.3 percent in 2013 (as measured by the change from the fourth quarter of the previous year) and by 3.3 percent in 2014. Economic growth is then projected to pick up further, and the economy is projected to reach its productive capacity in 2017 and continue to grow in line with the increase in that capacity thereafter. According to CBO's estimates, Path 1, which would increase deficits in comparison to the budgetary outcomes under current law, would increase output in the next few years and decrease it in later years compared with the economic outcomes under current law. Paths 2 and 3, which would reduce deficits, would reduce output in the next few years and increase it in later years compared with current-law economic outcomes.

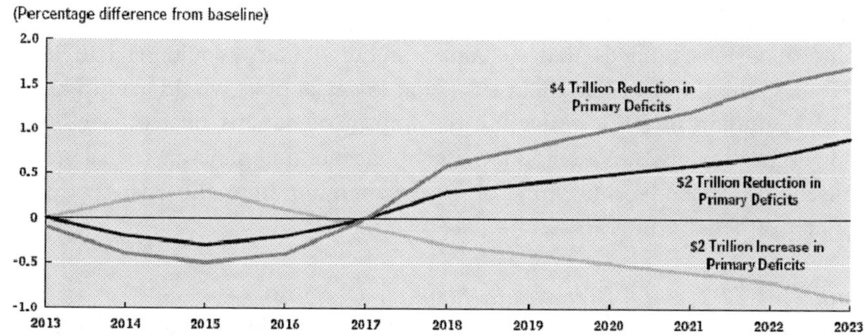

Source: Congressional Budget Office.

Notes: The illustrative paths are described in detail in the text, at the beginning of the section titled "Budget Deficits Under Three Illustrative Paths."

The primary deficit equals revenues minus noninterest spending.

Figures reflect the percentage difference in the annual levels between a path's effects and the outcomes under CBO's baseline, which incorporates the assumption that current laws generally remain unchanged.

Real GNP = inflation-adjusted gross national product.

Figure 2. Effects of Illustrative Paths on Real GNP, Calendar Years 2013 to 2023, Relative to Projections Under Current Law.

Those estimated effects on output incorporate the impact of the paths on interest rates. Under Path 1, interest rates would rise, and those effects would become larger over time—primarily because deficits under Path 1 would be larger than those under current law, and the resulting reduction in national saving would raise the returns on capital investments. Under Paths 2 and 3, interest rates would be lower than those under current law, and those effects would become larger over time, reflecting increasing deficit reduction.

For all of the paths, the effects on output and interest rates at the end of the coming decade would generally continue to grow in later years. However, those longer-term effects would depend on the precise way that policies were extended after 2023.

Effects on Gross National Product from 2014 to 2023

CBO estimates that, relative to current law, policies that raised spending and cut taxes would lead to higher deficits and higher GNP from 2014 to 2016, and policies that cut spending and raised taxes would lead to lower deficits and lower GNP from 2014 to 2016, reflecting the short-term impact of tax and spending policies on the demand for goods and services (see Figure 2). By contrast, CBO estimates that sustained higher deficits would lead to lower GNP beginning in 2017 and that sustained lower deficits would lead to higher GNP beginning in 2017, reflecting the impact of deficits on national saving and domestic investment (and without accounting for any changes to households' incentives to work or save stemming from the changes to tax policies or benefit programs).

Path 1: A $2 Trillion Increase in Primary Deficits

Because CBO estimates that the unspecified policies increasing the deficit by $2 trillion relative to that under current law would increase aggregate demand in the near term, real GNP would be 0.3 percent higher in the fourth quarter of 2014 than the amount under current law (see Table 1 on page 4).

That figure represents CBO's central estimate, which is based on the assumption that the values for key aspects of economic behavior (in particular, the extent to which higher aggregate demand brought about by the unspecified policies would lead to further changes in the economy) are the midpoints of estimated ranges. The full ranges that CBO uses for those parameters suggest that real GNP would be between 0.1 percent and 0.5 percent higher in the fourth quarter of 2014 than the amount under current law. However, the macroeconomic impact of changes in fiscal policy could lie outside the ranges of estimates reported here for this path as well as the others, depending on the future state of the economy, the responses of households and businesses to the policies, and numerous other factors.

In 2023, real GNP would be 0.9 percent lower than that under current law (or between 0.5 percent and 1.3 percent lower, under CBO's full range of assumptions). Larger deficits would reduce national saving and "crowd out" domestic investment (as savings that would otherwise fund private investment were instead used to purchase government debt)—lowering output. However, even with the negative impact of fiscal policy under this path, real GNP per person would be considerably higher in 2023 than it is now because of continued growth in labor productivity (see Figure 3).

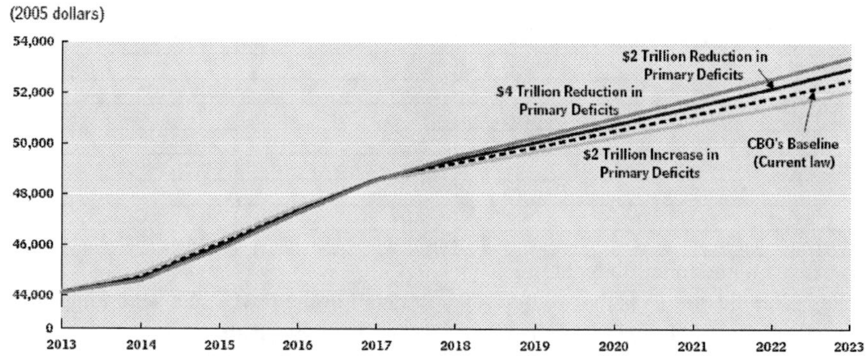

Source: Congressional Budget Office.

Notes: The illustrative paths are described in detail in the text, at the beginning of the section titled "Budget Deficits Under Three Illustrative Paths."

The primary deficit equals revenues minus noninterest spending.

Real GNP = inflation-adjusted gross national product.

Figure 3. Real GNP per Person Under CBO's Baseline and Illustrative Paths, Calendar Years 2014 to 2023.

Path 2: A $2 Trillion Reduction in Primary Deficits

By CBO's estimates, the unspecified policies reducing the deficit by $2 trillion relative to that under current law would decrease aggregate demand in the near term. As a result, real GNP would be 0.3 percent lower in the fourth quarter of 2014 than the amount under current law, CBO projects (or between 0.1 percent and 0.5 percent lower under CBO's full range of assumptions).

In 2023, real GNP would be 0.9 percent higher than the outcome under current law (or between 0.5 percent and 1.3 percent higher under CBO's full range of assumptions), as the effects of Path 1 are reversed: Smaller deficits would increase national saving and boost domestic investment, raising output.

Path 3: A $4 Trillion Reduction in Primary Deficits

Under this path, the effects on output would be double those under Path 2 because of the greater reduction in deficits. Real GNP would be 0.6 percent lower in the fourth quarter of 2014 than the amount under current law (or between 0.2 percent and 1.0 percent lower under CBO's full range of assumptions).

Table 3. Effects of Illustrative Paths on Interest Rates on 10-Year Treasury Notes in Selected Calendar Years, Relative to Projections under Current Law; (Percentage-point difference)

	Short Term (2014)	Longer Term (2023)
$2 Trillion Increase in Primary Deficits		
Central estimate	*	0.1
Range	* to 0.1	0.1 to 0.2
$2 Trillion Reduction in Primary Deficits		
Central estimate	*	-0.1
Range	*	-0.2 to -0.1
$4 Trillion Reduction in Primary Deficits		
Central estimate	-0.1	-0.2
Range	-0.1 to *	-0.4 to -0.1

Source: Congressional Budget Office.

Notes: The illustrative paths are described in detail in the text, at the beginning of the section titled "Budget Deficits Under Three Illustrative Paths."

The primary deficit equals revenues minus noninterest spending.

Figures reflect the percentage-point difference (in the fourth quarter levels) between a path's effects and the outcomes under CBO's baseline, which incorporates the assumption that current laws generally remain unchanged.

Ranges of estimated effects are shown to reflect the uncertainty that exists about many of the economic relationships that are important in the models used to calculate those effects.

The effects on rates of an increase in the deficit are larger than those of an equal-sized decrease in the deficit. See Appendix A for details.

* = between -0.05 and 0.05.

In 2023, real GNP would be 1.7 percent higher than the amount under current law (or between 0.9 percent and 2.5 percent higher under CBO's full range of assumptions). Particularly relevant for this path, a reduction of $4 trillion in the cumulative primary deficit relative to what would occur under current law would be very difficult to accomplish without directly changing incentives to work and save.

Effects on 10-Year Treasury Interest Rates from 2014 to 2023

Path 1 would tend to increase interest rates relative to CBO's baseline projections through two main channels. First, the path implies a higher cumulative deficit over the next 10 years than the outcome under current law.

Table 4. Effects of Illustrative Paths on the Cumulative Deficit for Fiscal Years 2014 to 2023, With and Without Economic Effects, Relative to Projections Under Current Law (Billions of dollars)

	Cumulative Deficit without Economic Effects	Cumulative Budgetary Impact of Economic Effects	Cumulative Deficit with Economic Effects
	Increases (-) in Deficits		
$2 Trillion Increase in Primary Deficits			
Effect on primary deficits	-2,000	-71	-2,071
Debt service	-322	-79	-401
Effect on total deficits	-2,322	-151	-2,472
	Decreases (+) in Deficits		
$2 Trillion Reduction in Primary Deficits			
Effect on primary deficits	2,000	47	2,047
Debt service	322	57	378
Effect on total deficits	2,322	103	2,425
$4 Trillion Reduction in Primary Deficits			
Effect on primary deficits	4,000	92	4,092
Debt service	643	94	737
Effect on total deficits	4,643	186	4,829

Source: Congressional Budget Office.

Notes: The illustrative paths are described in detail in the text, at the beginning of the section titled "Budget Deficits Under Three Illustrative Paths."

The primary deficit equals revenues minus noninterest spending. Debt service is the change in the deficit that would result from changes in the amount of interest paid on the public debt (including the effects of changes in interest rates). The effect on total deficits is the sum of the effects on primary deficits and debt service.

Negative numbers indicate that deficits under the path are larger than those under CBO's baseline, which incorporates the assumption that current laws generally remain unchanged; positive amounts indicate that deficits are smaller.

The effects on output and interest rates of an increase in the deficit are larger than those of an equal-sized decrease in the deficit. As a result, the budgetary impact of the economic effects is greater for Path 1 than for Path 2. In addition, the effects of a bigger decrease in the deficit are proportionally smaller than the effects of a smaller decrease. See Appendix A for details.

That higher cumulative deficit would lead to higher long-term interest rates every year because investment would be crowded out. Second, compared with current law, Path 1 would induce greater economic activity in the near term, which would lead the Federal Reserve to raise short-term interest rates somewhat sooner and to scale back other policies holding down long-term interest rates. As a result, the interest rate on 10-year Treasury securities would be a touch higher in 2014 than the rate under current law and 0.1 percentage point higher in 2023 (or as much as 0.2 percentage points higher under CBO's full range of assumptions) (see Table 3). Paths 2 and 3 would have the opposite effects, resulting in lower interest rates than those under current law. Under Path 2, the interest rate on 10-year Treasury securities would be a bit lower than that under current law in 2014 and 0.1 percentage point lower in 2023 (or as much as 0.2 percentage points lower under CBO's full range of assumptions). Under Path 3, the interest rate on 10-year Treasury securities would be 0.1 percentage point lower than that under current law in 2014 and 0.2 percentage points lower in 2023 (or between 0.1 percentage point and 0.4 percentage points lower under CBO's full range of assumptions).

THE BUDGETARY IMPACT OF THE MACROECONOMIC EFFECTS

The economic effects described above would "feed back" to the budget and affect the size of deficits. CBO has estimated those implications for the budget over fiscal years 2014 to 2023 using a simplified analysis that takes into account changes in taxable incomes and interest rates, among other things, but does not incorporate a detailed program-by-program analysis, as do CBO's regular budget projections. Most of the estimated effects that the paths would have on the budget stem from two factors:

- Changes in output would affect revenues by altering the amount of taxable incomes and
- Changes in deficits and thus the amount of debt (because of that change in revenues) and changes in interest rates would affect the federal government's interest payments, often known as debt service.

However, CBO's estimates also account for other effects, such as the impact of changes in prices on federal spending on purchases and transfer payments; the impact of the unemployment rate on federal spending on unemployment benefits; and the impact of the mix of taxable incomes on revenues.

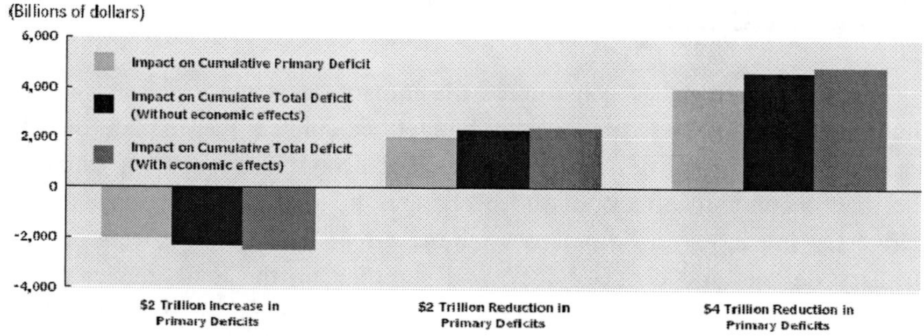

Source: Congressional Budget Office.

Notes: The illustrative paths are described in detail in the text, at the beginning of the section titled "Budget Deficits Under Three Illustrative Paths."

The primary deficit equals revenues minus noninterest spending. Debt service is the change in the deficit that would result from changes in the amount of interest paid on the public debt (including the effects of changes in interest rates). The effect on total deficits is the sum of the effects on primary deficits and debt service.

Negative numbers indicate that deficits under the path are larger than those under CBO's baseline, which incorporates the assumption that current laws generally remain unchanged; positive amounts indicate that deficits are smaller.

Figure 4. Effects of Illustrative Paths on the Cumulative Deficit for Fiscal Years 2014 to 2023, With and Without Economic Effects, Relative to Projections Under Current Law.

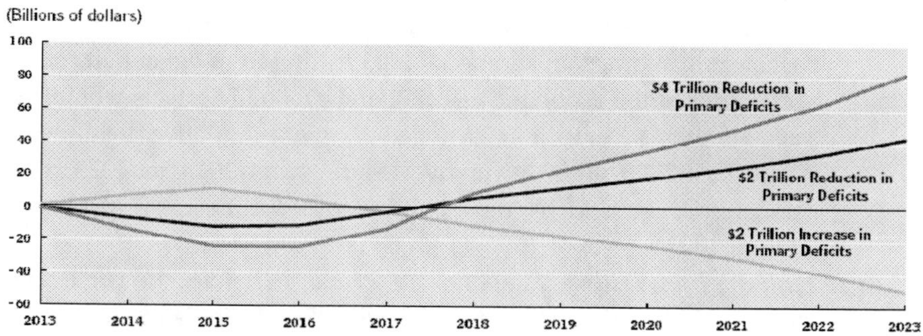

Source: Congressional Budget Office.

Notes: The illustrative paths are described in detail in the text, at the beginning of the section titled "Budget Deficits Under Three Illustrative Paths."

The primary deficit equals revenues minus noninterest spending. Debt service is the change in the deficit that would result from changes in the amount of interest paid on the public debt (including the effects of changes in interest rates). The budgetary impact of economic effects is the sum of the effects on primary deficits and debt service.

Negative numbers indicate that deficits under the path are larger than those under CBO's baseline, which incorporates the assumption that current laws generally remain unchanged; positive amounts indicate that deficits are smaller.

Figure 5. Budgetary Impact of Economic Effects of Illustrative Paths, Fiscal Years 2013 to 2023, Relative to Projections Under Current Law.

Cumulative Effects

For each path, CBO constructed the impact on primary deficits without including economic effects on the budget; calculated the impact on debt service and thus total deficits (again without economic feedback); estimated the macroeconomic effects of those changes in total deficits; estimated the budgetary impact of those macroeconomic effects (including effects on both primary deficits and debt service); and summed up the total impact on the budget, including debt service and economic effects, over fiscal years 2014 to 2023. The results are the following:

- *Path 1: A $2 Trillion Increase in Primary Deficits.* Additional debt service would add a cumulative $0.3 trillion to the budgetary cost over that period (before accounting for the economic effects), and economic effects would add $0.2 trillion (see Table 4). Altogether, the cumulative total deficit would be $2.5 trillion higher over fiscal years 2014 to 2023, CBO estimates (see Figure 4). As a result, debt held by the public would rise to 87 percent of GDP in 2023, compared with 73 percent at the end of fiscal year 2012 and 77 percent projected for 2023 under current law.
- *Path 2: A $2 Trillion Reduction in Primary Deficits.* Lower interest costs would subtract an additional $0.3 trillion from the deficit (before accounting forthe economic effects), and economic effects would subtract another $0.1 trillion. Altogether, the cumulative total deficit would be $2.4 trillion lower over fiscal years 2014 to 2023, CBO estimates. Debt held by the public would decline to 67 percent of GDP in 2023.
- *Path 3: A $4 Trillion Reduction in Primary Deficits.* Lower interest costs would subtract an additional $0.6 trillion from the deficit (before accounting for the economic effects), and economic effects would subtract $0.2 trillion. All told, the cumulative total deficit would be $4.8 trillion lower over fiscal years 2014 to 2023, CBO estimates. Debt held by the public would decline to 58 percent of GDP in 2023.

Differences in Impact over Time

The impact of economic effects on the budget would vary over time because of the different magnitude of the changes in the deficit and the projected improvement in the economy over time (under current law and any of the paths). In the short term under Path 1, output would be higher than that under current law, short-term interest rates would remain close to zero, and long-term interest rates would be little changed. Together, those short-term economic effects of Path 1 would reduce budget deficits in the next few years. For example, under Path 1, although the policy change without economic effects would boost the deficit by $40 billion in 2014, the economic effects of that change would offset about $7 billion of that increase. (See Figure 5; for additional detail on those effects and for estimates of the annual budgetary changes under each path, with and without economic effects, see Appendix B.)

Paths 2 and 3 would have similar short-term effects in the opposite direction. They would reduce output in the short run, and their economic effects would therefore tend to increase budget deficits in the next few years. For example, the economic effects of the budget policies under Path 2 would increase the deficit by $7 billion in fiscal year 2014, offsetting a portion of the $40 billion reduction assumed in the primary deficit; the economic effects of the budget policies under Path 3 would increase the total deficit by $14 billion in fiscal year 2014.

In the longer term, budgetary feedback effects would be driven primarily by changes in the cumulative deficit. A larger cumulative deficit such as that under Path 1 would tend to reduce output, with corresponding effects on taxable incomes. In addition, a larger deficit would tend to reduce national saving and thereby reduce the ratio of capital to labor, which would increase interest rates and thereby raise interest costs. Those factors would tend to worsen budget outcomes in later years under Path 1. Paths 2 and 3, which would reduce the cumulative deficit, would produce economic effects that improved budget outcomes over the longer term.

Economic and budgetary effects of fiscal policy are partly determined by the speed with which fiscal policy affects taxes and spending over time. For Paths 2 and 3, CBO chose budgetary paths that would reduce deficits by gradually rising amounts relative to those under current law, beginning in 2014. Of course, different timing for changes in budget policies is possible. The longer that significant deficit reduction is deferred, the larger the government's accumulated debt will be (with its associated costs and risks), and the greater the policy changes will need to be when deficit reduction begins. Conversely, the sooner that the deficit is cut, the more the economic effects will be felt when the economy is still relatively weak, and the less time that households, businesses, and state and local governments will have to plan and adjust their behavior. In addition, the timing of the steps taken to put fiscal policy on a sustainable course will affect different generations differently.

APPENDIX A: HOW CBO ESTIMATED THE ECONOMIC AND BUDGETARY EFFECTS OF THE ILLUSTRATIVE PATHS

The Congressional Budget Office (CBO) used two approaches to estimate the effects of the illustrative paths on the economy relative to the agency's baseline projections. Those approaches focus on somewhat different aspects of the economy and reflect distinct ways of thinking about it. One approach addresses short-term effects that stem largely from variations in aggregate demand; the other addresses medium-term and long-term effects on the economy's potential output. Each approach represents people's economic decisions in a simplified way while capturing some important aspects of actual behavior.

In CBO's judgment, the macroeconomic effects of the paths would be determined primarily by effects on the demand for goods and services in 2014, by effects on the nation's capital stock (including such things as factories and computers) and the labor supply in 2018 and beyond, and by a combination of those factors from 2015 through 2017.[1] CBO has estimated the economic effects of the paths relative to the agency's February 2013 baseline economic forecast, which incorporates the assumption that current laws generally remain in place.[2]

Short-Term Economic Effects

CBO analyzes the short-term economic effects of changes in fiscal policy by using models and historical evidence to estimate the direct and indirect effects of budget policies on the economy. Direct effects change output by influencing the demand for goods and services, by either the federal government or the people and organizations directly affected by a policy—for example, the recipients of a tax cut. The size of a direct effect depends on a tax or spending provision's impact on the behavior of recipients. For example, if someone receives a tax reduction of a dollar and spends 80 cents (saving the other 20 cents), and production increases over time to meet the additional demand generated by that spending, the direct impact on output is 80 cents.

The size of the direct effect, per dollar of budgetary cost, varies depending on the persistence of a policy (for example, whether it is permanent or temporary) and the characteristics of those affected by the policy (for example, whether the recipient of a tax cut or transfer has high or low income); in general, direct effects per dollar of budgetary cost are between zero and 1.0.[3]

Indirect effects enhance or offset direct effects. For example, the direct effects of lower taxes or higher spending are magnified when stronger demand for goods and services prompts companies to increase investment. In the other direction, direct effects are muted if higher government borrowing caused by tax decreases or spending increases leads to higher interest rates that discourage spending by households and businesses. With a large amount of unused resources in the U.S. economy today and over the next few years, CBO estimates that the indirect effects probably enhance the direct effects, on balance. Those additional effects can be represented by a demand multiplier, defined as the total change in output per dollar of direct effect on demand. Because there is considerable uncertainty about the economic relationships underlying indirect effects, CBO used estimates of that demand multiplier under current economic conditions ranging from 0.5 to 2.5, with a central estimate of 1.5, encompassing a broad range of economists' views.[4]

In addition, CBO made particular assumptions for the effects of the unspecified budgetary changes in the illustrative paths. CBO's analysis allowed those changes to have a range of effects on output. The medium-sized response reflects the assumption that each budgetary change of $1 would result in a direct effect of 67 cents and, including indirect effects, would change output cumulatively by $1 over several quarters.[5] At one end of the range, each $1 increase in the deficit was assumed to cause economic output to rise by a cumulative $0.33. At the opposite end of the range, each $1 increase in the deficit was assumed to cause economic output to rise by a cumulative $1.67. The monetary policy of the Federal Reserve has an important influence on the economic effects of changes in taxes and government spending. CBO's estimates in this analysis incorporate the assumption that over the next several years, with short-term interest rates near zero, unemployment elevated, and inflation low, the Federal Reserve's response to changes in fiscal policy will be limited. That assumption implies that the short-run impact of fiscal policy on the economy is larger than would be the case under more usual economic conditions, when, for example, the Federal Reserve would probably increase short-term interest rates in response to cuts in taxes or increases in government spending. A higher cumulative deficit over the long term under Path 1 would tend to boost long-term interest rates relative to those under current law as a higher cumulative deficit crowded out national saving available for investment. That effect would reduce the ratio of capital to labor in the economy in the long run, which would tend to increase the return on capital investments and, therefore, interest rates. Those long-run implications imply changes in interest rates even in the short run; long-term interest rates reflect, to at least some extent, the expectations that participants in financial markets have about future short-term rates. As a result, the expectation of an increase in interest rates as much as a decade in the future raises the interest rate on 10-year Treasury securities today. Policies that increased deficits over the next decade would engender such a reaction. In addition, the Federal Reserve would respond in a way that would increase longterm interest rates a little relative to the rates in CBO's baseline projections in the near term and thereby slightly attenuate the positive near-term economic effects of those policies. Because Paths 2 and 3 would reduce deficits, they would have the opposite effects on long-run interest rates in both the short run and the long run.

Fiscal policies might also affect spending by individuals and businesses by altering people's uncertainty or confidence about future economic conditions or government policies. Many firms appear to be uncertain today about future demand for their products, and that uncertainty seems to be leading them to be cautious about increasing their investment and hiring. Fiscal policy actions that would boost demand might lessen that uncertainty and increase employment.[6] However, such actions might also increase uncertainty about longer-run fiscal policy, which could have an opposing effect. Because quantifying such reactions to changes in fiscal policy would be extremely difficult, this report does not incorporate them.

Although the details of the changes to deficits under the illustrative paths in this report are not specified, the paths reflect the assumption that the underlying fiscal policies are credible, putting aside the effects of any potential doubts regarding the policies. Nevertheless, it is worth noting that households, businesses, state and local governments, and participants in the financial markets would be more likely to believe that intended deficit reduction would truly take effect in the future if specific and widely supported policy changes were enacted into law in advance.

Medium-Term and Long-Term Economic Effects

In estimating the effects of deficits beyond the next few years, CBO uses an enhanced version of a widely used model developed by Robert Solow. In that model, output depends on the quantity and quality of the labor force, the size and composition of the capital stock, and the nation's technological progress.[7]

This analysis focused on how the illustrative paths would affect output and income by changing the nation's capital stock (through the magnitude of deficits) and the labor supply (through the pretax wage rate). For example, a path leading to projected debt higher than that implied by current law would tend to generate lower output and higher interest rates because of crowding out of capital investment. That reduction in capital investment would, in turn, lower pretax wage rates.

The capital stock owned by residents of the United States depends on national saving, which is the sum of personal saving, business saving (that is, after-tax corporate profits not paid as dividends), and saving or dissaving (as reflected in budget surpluses or deficits) by the federal government and state and local governments. Federal budget deficits reduce national saving, resulting in a smaller capital stock owned by U.S. residents over time from a decrease in domestic investment, an increase in net borrowing from abroad, or both. To reflect the high degree of uncertainty that attends those effects, CBO produced estimates of the economic effects of the illustrative paths using a range of assumptions about how each dollar increase in deficits would reduce domestic investment (reflecting different assumptions about the effects of deficits on both national saving and net borrowing from abroad):

- A "large" investment response, under which each dollar increase in deficits would reduce domestic investment by 50 cents;
- A "small" investment response, under which each dollar increase in deficits would reduce domestic investment by 15 cents; and
- A "medium" investment response, under which each dollar increase in deficits would reduce domestic investment by 33 cents.

The smaller capital stock that results from less investment would decrease economic output (because the labor force would have less capital and would therefore be less productive) and increase interest rates (because the greater scarcity of capital would drive up the cost of using it).

Productive investments by the government can also increase output by raising productivity in the private sector. However, the unspecified changes in deficits that differentiate the three paths were assumed to leave government investment unchanged.

To reflect the high degree of uncertainty that attends the effect of the wage rate on the supply of labor, CBO produced estimates of the economic effects of the illustrative budgetary paths using a range of assumptions about how people would adjust the number of hours they worked in response to changes in the wage rate:

- A "strong" labor supply response, under which workers' response is on the high side of the range of empirical estimates;
- A "weak" labor supply response, under which workers' response is on the low side of the range; and
- A "medium" labor supply response, under which workers' response is roughly midway between strong and weak.

The responsiveness of the labor supply to wages is often expressed as the total wage elasticity (the change in total labor income caused by a 1 percent change in after-tax wages). The total wage elasticity, in turn, has two components: a substitution elasticity, which measures the effect of changes in the amount of additional income from each additional hour of work (applicable to an additional dollar of income) and an income elasticity, which measures the effect of changes in total income (the total tax liability divided by income). In this analysis, CBO's assumptions for the labor supply response correspond to total wage elasticities of about 0.32 for the strong response (composed of a substitution elasticity of 0.32 and an income elasticity of zero); about 0.06 for the weak response (composed of a substitution elasticity of 0.16 and an income elasticity of -0.10); and about 0.19 for the medium response (composed of a substitution elasticity of 0.24 and an income elasticity of -0.05).[8]

Asymmetries in Economic and Budgetary Effects

In the long run, an increase in deficits affects output more than does an equal-sized decrease, CBO estimates. Each additional increment to the capital stock raises GDP by a smaller amount. Consequently, even though positive and negative changes to the deficit are estimated to have symmetrical direct effects on capital investment, the resulting effects on output are not symmetrical: An increase in deficits (which shrinks the capital stock) has a proportionally greater effect on output than does an equal-sized reduction in deficits. (For the same reason, Path 3, under which the initial reduction in primary deficits is twice as large as that of Path 2, has effects on output that are less than twice as large.)

Similarly, an increase in deficits has a greater effect on interest rates than does an equal-sized decrease, for two reasons. First, with short-term interest rates currently near zero, they are more readily boosted by an increase in deficits than they are dampened by a decrease in deficits. Moreover, the bigger differences in the path of short-term rates after an increase in deficits imply bigger changes in long-term rates, even before those short-term rates begin to change. Second, the interest rate is more responsive to changes in the capital stock as the capital stock gets smaller. As a result, an increase in deficits has a proportionally larger effect on interest rates. (For the same reason, under Path 3, the effects on interest rates are less than twice as large as those under Path 2.)

The asymmetry in economic effects implies an asymmetry in budgetary effects. Higher deficits reduce output, and therefore taxable incomes, to a greater degree than lower deficits increase them; and higher deficits increase interest rates, and therefore interest payments, by more than lower deficits decrease them. Therefore, the economic effects of higher deficits boost the deficit by a greater increment than the economic effects of lower deficits shrink the deficit. Over time, those budgetary effects, in turn, further affect the capital stock, magnifying the initial difference in the effects on output and interest rates.

Differences from Previous Estimates of Economic Effects

The estimated economic effects of a $2 trillion reduction in primary deficits presented in this report differ slightly from those CBO presented in July 2011 for several reasons.[9] First, on the basis of a continuing review of the evidence, CBO reduced its estimate of the "medium" investment response from 36 cents per dollar of deficit to 33 cents per dollar of deficit and reduced its "small" investment response from 20 cents per dollar of deficit to 15 cents per dollar of deficit. As a result of those revisions, both the central and most favorable estimates of the impact of reduced deficits on gross national product (GNP) are smaller than previously estimated.

In addition, for the current analysis, CBO assumed that deficit reduction would be phased in more slowly than was assumed in the 2011 report. That difference implies a smaller cumulative reduction in interest payments, also leading to a smaller estimated effect of deficit reduction on GNP.

Budgetary Impact of the Macroeconomic Effects

CBO estimated the budgetary implications of the macroeconomic effects of the illustrative paths using a simplified analysis that takes into account changes in taxable incomes and interest rates, among other things, but does not incorporate a detailed program-by-program analysis, as occurs for CBO's regular budget projections.

Most of the estimated impact of the economic effects on the budget stems from changes in taxable incomes and interest rates.

Changes in output affect the budget through their impact on taxable incomes: Higher output implies higher taxable incomes—increasing revenues and reducing the deficit.

In addition, economic growth can push taxpayers into higher tax brackets, so revenues tend to rise more than proportionally with taxable incomes. CBO's budget calculations for this analysis reflect features of U.S. tax laws that result in little U.S. tax effectively being imposed on foreign income of U.S. residents and much of the income earned in this country by foreign residents effectively being taxed here.

Interest rates affect the budget mostly through their impact on the government's interest payments on the national debt. But changes in interest rates are reflected in total interest costs only gradually, as new securities are issued at those higher rates.

New securities must be sold to pay for the redemption of maturing securities and to finance additional borrowing because of larger deficits. Currently, about 23 percent of marketable federal debt held by the public has a maturity of two years or less.

APPENDIX B: FURTHER DETAILS ON ECONOMIC AND BUDGETARY EFFECTS

In this appendix, the Congressional Budget Office's (CBO's) estimate of the effects of each illustrative path on the primary deficit, net interest, and total deficits are shown relative to the projected outcomes under current law with economic effects included (see Table B-1).

The differences between the estimates with and without economic effects included constitute the budgetary impact of the economic effects (see Table B-2).

Table B-1. Effects of Illustrative Paths on the Budget with Economic Effects, Fiscal Years 2014 to 2023, Relative to Projections under Current Law (Billions of dollars)

	2014	2015	2016	2017	2018	2019	2020	2021	2022	2023	2014-2023
	Increases (-) in Deficits										
$2 Trillion Increase in Primary Deficits											
Effect on primary deficits	-33	-64	-103	-145	-188	-229	-268	-307	-347	-388	-2,071
Debt service	[1]	-2	-7	-14	-25	-35	-49	-67	-88	-113	-401
Effect on Total Deficits	-34	-65	-110	-159	-213	-264	-317	-375	-436	-501	-2,472
	Decreases (+) in Deficits										
$2 Trillion Reduction in Primary Deficits											
Effect on primary deficits	33	63	99	141	185	226	265	304	345	386	2,047
Debt service	1	1	5	12	23	33	47	64	85	108	378
Effect on Total Deficits	33	65	104	153	208	259	312	369	429	494	2,425
$4 Trillion Reduction in Primary Deficits											
Effect on primary deficits	65	126	197	278	370	453	531	610	690	772	4,092
Debt service	2	3	9	21	42	64	92	127	166	212	737
Effect on Total Deficits	67	129	206	299	412	517	623	736	856	984	4,829
Memorandum:											
CBO's February 2013 Baseline											
Primary deficit (-) or surplus	-373	-158	-153	-123	-88	-117	-131	-123	-163	-120	-1,549
Net interest (-)	-243	-272	-323	-412	-517	-593	-667	-730	-795	-857	-5,410
Total Deficit	-616	-430	-476	-535	-605	-710	-798	-854	-957	-978	-6,958

Source: Congressional Budget Office.

Notes: The illustrative paths are described in detail in the text, at the beginning of the section titled "Budget Deficits Under Three Illustrative Paths."

The primary deficit equals revenues minus noninterest spending. Debt service is the change in the deficit that would result from changes in the amount of interest paid on the public debt (including the effects of changes in interest rates). The effect on total deficits is the sum of the effect on primary deficits and debt service.

Negative numbers indicate that deficits under the path are larger than those under CBO's baseline, which incorporates the assumption that current laws generally remain unchanged; positive amounts indicate that deficits are smaller.

The effects on output and interest rates of an increase in the deficit are larger than those of an equal-sized decrease in the deficit. As a result, the budgetary impact of the economic effects is greater for Path 1 and for Path 2. See Appendix A for details.

Table B-2. Budgetary Impact of Economic Effects of Illustrative Paths, Fiscal Years 2014 to 2023, Relative to Projections Under Current Law (Billions of dollars)

	2014	2015	2016	2017	2018	2019	2020	2021	2022	2023	2014-2023
	Increases (-) / Decreases (+) in Deficits										
$2 Trillion Increase in Primary Deficits											
Effect on primary deficits	7	12	8	2	-6	-11	-14	-18	-23	-28	-71
Debt service	-1	-1	-3	-5	-5	-6	-9	-12	-16	-22	-79
Effect on Total Deficits	7	11	5	-3	-11	-17	-23	-30	-39	-50	-151
$2 Trillion Reduction in Primary Deficits											
Effect on primary deficits	-7	-12	-12	-5	3	8	12	16	20	26	47
Debt service	1	1	1	2	3	4	6	9	13	17	57
Effect on Total Deficits	-7	-12	-11	-3	6	12	18	25	33	43	103
$4 Trillion Reduction in Primary Deficits											
Effect on primary deficits	-15	-25	-26	-15	6	17	24	32	41	52	92
Debt service	1	2	2	2	3	6	10	16	22	30	94
Effect on Total Deficits	-14	-24	-24	-13	9	23	35	48	63	82	186

Source: Congressional Budget Office.

Notes: The illustrative paths are described in detail in the text, at the beginning of the section titled "Budget Deficits Under Three Illustrative Paths."

The primary deficit equals revenues minus noninterest spending. Debt service is the change in the deficit that would result from changes in the amount of interest paid on the public debt (including the effects of changes in interest rates). The effect on total deficits is the sum of the effects on primary deficits and debt service.

Negative numbers indicate that deficits under the path are larger than those under CBO's baseline, which incorporates the assumption that current laws generally remain unchanged; positive amounts indicate that deficits are smaller.

The effects on output and interest rates of an increase in the deficit are larger than those of an equal-sized decrease in the deficit. As a result, the budgetary impact of the economic effects is greater for Path 1 and for Path 2. See Appendix A for details.

The estimated effects of each path on gross domestic product (GDP) are shown for 2014 and 2023 relative to the projected outcomes under current law (see Table B-3). In general, the short-term effects are very similar to those on gross national product (GNP). In the longer run, the effects on GDP tend to be smaller than those on GNP. For example, according to CBO's central estimates, Path 3 would boost real (inflation-adjusted) GDP by 1.0 percent in 2023; in comparison, Path 3 would boost real GNP by 1.7 percent in 2023.

Table B-3. Effects of Illustrative Paths on Real GDP in Selected Calendar Years, Relative to Projections Under Current Law (Percentage difference)

	Short Term (2014)	Longer Term (2023)
$2 Trillion Increase in Primary Deficits		
Central estimate	0.3	-0.5
Range	0.1 to 0.5	-0.9 to -0.2
$2 Trillion Reduction in Primary Deficits		
Central estimate	-0.3	0.5
Range	-0.5 to -0.1	0.2 to 0.8
$4 Trillion Reduction in Primary Deficits		
Central estimate	-0.6	1.0
Range	-1.1 to -0.2	0.4 to 1.7

Source: Congressional Budget Office.

Notes: The illustrative paths are described in detail in the text, at the beginning of the section titled "Budget Deficits Under Three Illustrative Paths."

The primary deficit equals revenues minus noninterest spending.

Figures reflect the percentage difference in the fourth quarter levels between a path's effects and the outcomes under CBO's baseline, which incorporates the assumption that current laws generally remain unchanged.

Ranges of estimated effects are shown to reflect the uncertainty that exists about many of the economic relationships that are important in the models used to calculate those effects.

The effects on GDP of an increase in the deficit are larger than those of a decrease in the deficit. See Appendix A for details. Real GDP = inflation-adjusted gross domestic product.

The differences between the effects on GDP and GNP reflect the consequences of changes in profits and interest payments sent abroad. Consider the effects of smaller budget deficits. First, those smaller deficits would generate smaller inflows of capital from other countries; as a result, a smaller portion of the nation's income would have to be sent abroad as returns (in the form of profits or interest) on that invested capital and thus would not be available to U.S. households. Second, those smaller deficits would lower interest rates, implying lower payments for each dollar of foreign-owned U.S. assets. Both of those effects would have a positive impact on GNP that would not be included in GDP. Similarly, for larger budget deficits, the negative impact on GNP would be larger than the negative impact on GDP.

End Notes

[1] See Congressional Budget Office, The Budget and Economic Outlook: Fiscal Years 2013 to 2023 (February 2013).

[2] See, for instance, Congressional Budget Office, Choices for Deficit Reduction (November 2012).

[3] The effects on output and interest rates of an increase in the deficit are larger than those of an equal-sized decrease in the deficit. As a result, the overall budgetary impact (including economic effects) of Path 1 is greater than that of Path 2 despite the fact that they begin with the same cumulative change in primary deficits. See Appendix A for details.

[4] For examples of CBO's analysis of all of those effects of specific policies, see Congressional Budget Office, Economic Effects of Policies Contributing to Fiscal Tightening in 2013 (November 2012), The Long-Term Budget Outlook (June 2012), The Economic Impact of the President's 2013 Budget (April 2012), Policies for Increasing Growth and Employment in 2012 and 2013 (November 2011), and The Economic Outlook and Fiscal Policy Choices (September 2010).

[5] See Congressional Budget Office, Estimated Impact of the American Recovery and Reinvestment Act on Employment and Economic Output from July 2012 Through September 2012 (November 2012).

[6] For examples of such previous work, see Congressional Budget Office, The Economic Impact of the President's 2013 Budget (April 2012), and The Macroeconomic and Budgetary Effects of an Illustrative Policy for Reducing the Federal Budget Deficit (July 2011).

End Notes for Appendix A

[1] Specifically, CBO combines results from its modeling approaches as follows: estimates for 2013 and 2014 are based entirely on effects on demand; estimates for 2015, 2016, and 2017 place weights of 0.75, 0.50, and 0.25, respectively, on the effects on demand and the remaining weights on the effects on the capital stock and labor supply; and estimates for 2018 and beyond are based entirely on effects on the capital stock and labor supply.

[2] See Congressional Budget Office, *The Budget and Economic Outlook: Fiscal Years 2013 to 2023* (February 2013).

[3] For a review of the ranges of short-term economic impact that CBO estimates for different types of specific policies, see Congressional Budget Office, *Economic Effects of Policies Contributing to Fiscal Tightening in 2013* (November 2012).

[4] For a discussion of CBO's approach to analyzing the short-term effects of fiscal policy, see Felix Reichling and Charles Whalen, *Assessing the Short-Term Effects on Output of Changes in Federal Fiscal Policies*, Congressional Budget Office Working Paper 2012-08 (May 2012).

[5] For the purpose of this analysis, CBO assumed that 75 percent of the overall direct effect from unspecified budgetary changes would occur in the quarter when the change in the deficit occurred and 25 percent would occur in the following quarter.

[6] See Nicholas Bloom, "The Impact of Uncertainty Shocks," *Econometrica*, vol. 77, no. 3 (May 2009), pp. 623–685.

[7] For details of that model and a discussion of alternative assumptions about the effects of budget deficits on saving and investment, see Congressional Budget Office, *The Economic Impact of the President's 2013 Budget* (April 2012), Appendix A.

[8] For details on CBO's assumptions about the impact of the wage rate on the labor supply, see Congressional Budget Office, *How the Supply of Labor Responds to Changes in Fiscal Policy* (October 2012).

[9] Congressional Budget Office, *The Macroeconomic and Budgetary Effects of an Illustrative Policy for Reducing the Federal Budget Deficit* (July 2011).

INDEX

D

E

F

G

H

I